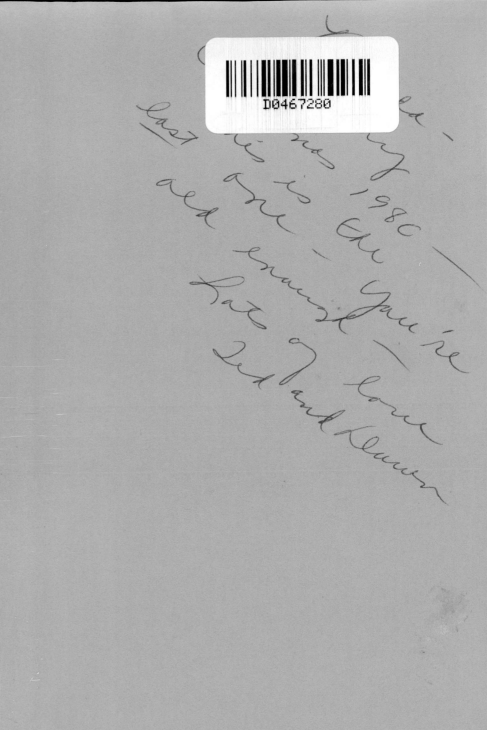

Moments to Remember

Moments to Remember

Collected by
CANDIDA LUND

THE THOMAS MORE PRESS
Chicago, Illinois

ISBN 0-88347-110-8

Acknowledgements

The compiler and publisher wish to thank the following for permission to reprint excerpts from the works listed below:

Benjamin Blom, Inc.: From LIFE OF MRS. SIDDONS (first published London, 1838) by Thomas Campbell. Reissued by Benjamin Blom, Inc. Distributed by Arno Press, Inc.

Channel Press: "I Wish for No Other Earth" by Florence Nightingale, from LETTERS TO MOTHER: AN ANTHOLOGY edited by Charles Van Doren. Copyright © 1959 by Charles Van Doren. Previously published in THE LIFE OF FLORENCE NIGHTINGALE by Sir Edward T. Cook, published by Macmillan and Company, Inc. 1913.

Coward-McCann, Inc.: From THE WHITE CLIFFS by Alice Duer Miller. Copyright © 1940 by Alice Duer Miller.

John Day Company: From THE CHILD WHO NEVER GREW by Pearl S. Buck. Copyright © 1950 by the Training School at Vineland, New Jersey.

Contents

(Note: names of fictional characters are *italicized*)

This volume is dedicated to women, dear to me, who have provided me with love, encouragement, inspiration and joy: Kitty, Eleanor, Mame, Ann, Doreen, Eppie, Marge, Polly, Mary Lou, Kathy, Peggy, Laurie, Mari, and all my Sisters—and those others who have touched my life.

Preface

"Remember to live," Goethe said. *Moments to Remember* tells of women who have remembered to live (although madness drove one to take her life). Primarily for that reason these women speak to all today. They tell of happiness and sorrow, triumph and discouragement.

Perhaps now more than at any other time we are asking what is happiness? Certainly it is loving and being loved, but how, where, how much? Is happiness always light-hearted? No, although real laughter can help. In *A Doll's House,* Helmer and Nora have this exchange:

> Helmer: Have you not been happy here?
> Nora: No, never, I thought I was, but I never was.
> Helmer: Not—not happy!
> Nora: No; only merry.

Is happiness different at different ages? At sixteen Sylvia Plath thought that she was "very happy." But a more mature Liv Ullmann wrote, "I believe that the overpowering happiness—when the whole world is fragrant and the sun shines and one is almost unconscious from emotion—I believe it comes less frequently."

In our world happiness appears fragile and often threatened. Perhaps that is one reason why the contemporary woman preoccupies herself with its quest. To help her she needs to know how other women have experienced happiness. She needs also to know how they have coped with sorrow and even tragedy. The human experience is a shared experience upon which we all are able to draw. And thus we grow.

This book is a reflection of that shared human experience. Every woman will find some experiences in it with which she can identify. She will be able to say to herself, "I've known that joy . . . that sorrow." Purposely the selections have not been placed in chronological order, nor by country of birth, nor any other tidy category. Yet the arrangement is not haphazard. It attempts to mirror life itself where joys and sorrows, laughter and grief alternate and where no century nor nation can claim more of the human drama. Most of the women are real; a few are fictitious, but these, too, reflect reality.

Although it is a book about women, it is not meant only for women. I hope that men also will find here a greater understanding of the joys and pains of being human.

I would be happy if this book gave some readers a measure of joy, or courage, or hope, or comfort, or laughter. These women deserve to be remembered.

CANDIDA LUND
Rosary College
River Forest, Illinois

Helen Hayes

Helen Hayes (1900–   ) was born in Washington, D.C., where she grew up. Her mother peppered her own domesticity with bouts of acting, so it was not surprising that her daughter first appeared professionally on the stage at the age of six.

She attended Holy Cross Academy and Sacred Heart Academy, and as Catholic academies in those days were a-hum with theatrical activities, she was continually performing in school productions. The proudest boast of the speech teacher at Sacred Heart, a member of my own religious order, was that she had taught Helen Hayes.

Looking back, Helen Hayes is uncertain whether her mother's fostering of her career strengthened or weakened her professionally. It kept her, in her opinion, from developing initiative and confidence, and resulted in timidity.

This timidity is seen in Helen Hayes' account of her first meeting with Charles MacArthur (whose best-known play, The Front Page, *was written with Ben Hecht). That meeting was the beginning of a great love, a love that makes it possible for her to say today, "How terrible it would have been to have missed my life with him." Certainly their marriage had regrettable moments—and sorrows—but as she has pointed out, these did not alter the larger truth: "Charlie MacArthur and I had found each other in the crowd—he never stopped calling me his bride. That miracle remains."*

I DIDN'T feel much like a star the day I met Charlie at Neysa McMein's studio on 57th Street. Marc Connelly had seen me on Fifth Avenue, and after I agreed to help him choose a gift for Margalo Gilmore, I unwillingly allowed him to drag me to one of the few legitimate salons in New York. I was starring in his play, *To the Ladies,* but knew few celebrities other than those with whom I might have been working. My friends were still to become famous and it was still possible to feel at ease with them.

Miss McMein's studio overwhelmed me, and so did she. Our hostess sat on a raised platform in a smock and beret, a warm and untidy person with tawny hair and a lazy, purring manner. She was like a tortoise-shell cat who had attended art school. She managed for years to retain the expectant quality of a young artist—about to arrive, on the threshold, always at the beginning. When I met her that afternoon, she sat before her easel working on a new cover for *Cosmopolitan Magazine,* ostensibly unaware of her glittering guests.

The large room fairly crawled with celebrity. Marc, as the latest arrival, took center stage, greeting one and all with a heartincss and enthusiasm that would never have suggested that he had seen everyone of these people the evening before.

Between four and seven every day, Miss McMein's marvelous sky-lighted studio was a must for the town's bright new talents. They were attracted like bees to honey and the constant buzz was of sweet success.

My entrance was not particularly hailed, and, after a few perfunctory introductions, I found a corner and sat drinking it all in. Slim, dark Irving Berlin was at the piano, resembling one of the black notes, and the exotic, prognathous George Gershwin was straining at the leash to replace him. Robert Benchley, an enchanted toad of a man, was croaking with laughter at a new joke Marc had just whispered to him, and the patrician Alice Duer Miller was monopolizing my idol of the moment, Shaw's *St. Joan*—the wonderful actress Winifred Lenihan. *To the Ladies'* co-author, George S. Kaufman, and his wife, Beatrice, carved for each other like primitive sculptures, dominated a large group of admirers; and the waspish Alexander Woollcott was, for the moment, smiling benignly, presiding over the honeycomb as if it were the Seventh Day and he had created it all and couldn't have been more pleased with the results.

I sipped my ginger ale and devoured the whole scene. It would have been the most exciting in my life, had I not been so painfully a part of it.

It was a stage set, and the most trivial utterance emerged as polished dialogue. No one ever just *said* anything there. Everyone was *on*—shining and outshining. I sat terrified that I would be asked the time of day and have to coin a bon mot in reply. This was not a room in which one could ever simply say "Six twenty." What a bore! I suppose "Everything is at sixes and sevens" might have given me high marks, but it has taken me 35 years to think of it and this crowd was a fast one and not in a waiting mood.

Since they were virtually all famous strangers to me, their gossip was way over my head. Snatches of conversations, tag lines of stories, esoteric references to soubriquetted friends would create a swell of uproarious mirth that was shared by all—except me. For fear that I might be thought a simpleton or stone-deaf or possibly both, I would occasionally cock my head with a knowing amusement or lower my eyelids in tolerant acceptance of the madness that prompted Dotty to say, "Really!" with such pith or provoked Harpo to insist, "You're slightly, Dotty!"

I didn't know what in tarnation anybody was talking about. Durable Irving—still at the piano—was playing his *Always* with one finger, like a little boy, and that lovely melody drifted toward me over the din along with the most beautiful young man I'd ever seen. He stood looking down at me with hazel eyes dabbed with green. His hair was curly, his ears pointed. This was a mouth designed exclusively for smiling. He looked exactly like a faun, though Brownie later informed me that from what she heard— and it was the most reliable of sources—he was worse; he was a "satire!"

"Do you want a peanut?" this enchanting creature asked.

My Charlie's life was composed almost entirely of brilliant curtain lines. Openers or closers, the mot juste, the phrase that would tie up a situation always outlived the crisis that inspired it. He was a writer, and his gift was regretted only once in his whole life. In his never-ending compulsion to live up to his legend he now found it necessary to invent a phrase that unfortunately proved deathless.

It wasn't enough that he poured the peanuts from a crumpled paper bag into my trembling hands. He had to add, "I wish they were emeralds."

Of course, I was bowled over. Starting with Mother, that evening, I told everyone who would listen all about it. When in Hollywood some years later, I wanted to be cooperative with an interviewer and I repeated it again, the line was committed to print. From that moment on, it was to haunt us. Even as late as our tenth anniversary, which we celebrated *à deux* at his favorite bistro, "21", we found a bowl of dyed-green peanuts awaiting us on our table, the artwork of the owners—the famous Jack and Charlie. Such antics over the years so depressed Charlie that, at the end of World War II, returning from India and the Eastern Theater, he dumped a bag of emeralds in my lap.

"I wish they were peanuts," was his only comment.

Charlie MacArthur! Playwright and playboy, reporter and soldier of fortune, blazing wit and the eternal, white-haired boy— my Charlie.

From *On Reflection* by Helen Hayes

Ann Landers

In the late seventies American newspaper editors chose the most influential woman in this country. Unerringly their choice was Eppie Lederer who writes as Ann Landers. In her daily column of counsel and encouragement her influence touches 70,000,000 readers. From its original spot in the Chicago Sun-Times *the column has fanned out, and now is syndicated in over a thousand newspapers.*

It was in 1955 that Eppie Lederer became Ann Landers as well. No one could be two persons with greater grace and deftness than Eppie Lederer. In part, perhaps this is because she so brims with vitality, ideas, and largesse of spirit that one could say it takes two personae to contain her.

More than a decade ago a recognized professor of political philosophy told me that in his opinion Ann Landers' writing more closely resembled Aristotle's Ethics *than that of any other contemporary writer. In her columns, Ann Landers emerges as a strong, confident, courageous woman. Fortunately the thrust of her columns has been continued further in a valuable volume,* The Ann Landers Encyclopedia, A to Z. *This is a book remarkable not only for its scope, but also for its prestigious contributors, many of whom are her personal friends and who would have written their articles only for her.* The Encyclopedia, *happily, is laced generously with excerpts from her own columns, and these provide some of the most insightful observations.*

Here I have chosen selections that are a departure from Ann Landers' usual columns in that they are extremely personal—and Eppie Lederer comes to the fore.

Dear Readers: This may be just another day to you, but it is a very special day in my life. Thirty years ago, on a sweltering

Sunday afternoon in Sioux City, Iowa, Jules Lederer slipped a plain gold band on my finger, and I became his wife.

Honesty forbids me describing myself as a student at Morningside College, so I'll simply say I was enrolled there. Jules had had one year at Northwestern—High School, that is. He was a product of Detroit, handsome, energetic, imaginative, a born optimist and eager to take on the world. He had a good job and a promising future. He was also broke.

I was an effervescent, fun-loving girl, hopelessly square, driven by a crusading spirit to save the world—sort of a Jewish Joan of Arc. I was engaged to marry a law student in California. But Jules, never one to be discouraged by small obstacles, asked me to marry him anyway. I said yes, and the wedding took place three months later.

We were blessed the following year with a baby girl, Margo. From then on, I saw more of the moving van than I saw of Jules. When an opportunity for advancement arose, he took it. And it seemed always to be in another city. We moved from Sioux City to St. Louis, from St. Louis to New Orleans, from New Orleans to Milwaukee. Then came World War II, and Jules served in the infantry. In 1945, we moved from Little Rock to Los Angeles, from Los Angeles to Eau Claire, Wis., and from Eau Claire to Chicago.

Time, that subtle thief of youth, is often cursed by those who long to stop the clock, or turn it back, but we want none of that. Each year has been better than the last because we have grown together. A good marriage, it is said, is made in heaven. This might be true, but the maintenance work must be done right down here. A successful marriage is not a gift, it is an achievement. No real marriage can exist without differences in opinion and the ensuing battles. But battles can be healthy. They bring to marriage the vital principle of equal partnership. If there is a secret to making marriage work it is "Never go to bed mad."

Our 30 years together have been blessed with good health,

good fortune, good friends, good times and success. Jules says he could not have made it without me. I am not sure he is right. But I could not have made it without him, and of THIS I am certain. He taught me how to be alone without feeling sorry for myself. He taught me never to back away from a challenge—that it is better to try and fail and then to try again. He taught me how to use my time productively. His work habits are impeccable. I learned mine from him.

Being Mrs. Jules Lederer has been superb training for Ann Landers. Thirty years with this unselfish, supportive, responsive man has enabled me to live life as few people get the opportunity to live it. Being Ann Landers' husband could pose a terrible problem, but Jules has met the challenge with dignity and incredible good humor. My husband is my best friend, and I am his. I consider it a privilege to be the wife of this beautiful guy, who took on the world with a ninth-grade education and a hole in his sock.

From "A Special Day for Our Ann Landers,"
Ask Ann Landers, July 2, 1969

Dear Readers: There will be no letters and answers in the column today. My heart is heavy, and I am not up to giving advice. Last night, I lost my lovely mother-in-law.

Gustie Lederer of Detroit passed away quietly in her sleep. She was 81. God gave her 11 years more than the Biblical three score and 10, which, according to the Scriptures, is the rich, full life. And rich and full it was. Gustie attended the weddings of nine grandchildren, and she lived to hold in her arms 10 great-grandchildren.

This remarkable little woman, only 4-foot-10, was widowed at the age of 37 when her husband was killed in an auto accident near Jackson, Mich. She was left with seven young children. My husband, Jules, was her eldest son. Jules knew what had to be done, and he did it. Immediately after his 16th birthday, he left high school to go to work and help support the family.

Gustie was no chicken-soup mama. She was loving and gentle, but she was also determined that her children be self-reliant and independent. There was neither the time nor money for pampering and multiple choices that so many children today find frustrating. Everyone did his share. Gustie once told me that she never set up any house rules and she had very few disciplinary problems. Her children knew what was expected of them, and they did it.

Not one of the seven went wrong, although, had they done so, the psychiatrists and psychologists could have come up with many plausible "explanations." The situation was classic—teenagers without a father, severe economic hardship, etc. "We were what you might call disadvantaged," Jules once told me, "but we weren't actually poor. We just didn't have any money."

Gustie was my mother-in-law for 34 years, and as God is my judge, we never exchanged one unpleasant word. Her five daughters, each one blessed with a delightful sense of humor, often chided me about being Gustie's "favorite." It was only natural, they allowed, since I had the good fortune to live in Chicago and they all lived in Detroit. Gustie called me "Eppeleh with the Keppeleh," which in Yiddish means, "Little Eppie with the good head." But there was more to our relationship than appeared on the surface. Apart from the obvious affection and many good laughs we enjoyed, there was a quiet understanding—my unspoken gratitude for the wonderful son she raised for me—and her deep appreciation for my being a good wife to him.

After her second attack of congestive heart failure, we knew the end was in sight. The time had come for Ann Landers to take some of her own advice. I telephoned the doctor in charge and asked that no extraordinary measures be used—no needles, no tubes, no machines that might deny Gustie the right to die with dignity. I asked that she be kept comfortable and left in God's hands. The doctor assured me that he was in complete accord, and he kept his word.

Fifteen years ago, I ran a contest in search of the world's best mother-in-law. The winner was a woman in Kansas City. Her nomination was sent in by her daughter's husband. The prize was a gold medal on which was engraved "To the World's Best Mother-in-law." When I sent the Kansas City woman her medal, I sent a duplicate medal to Gustie Lederer in Detroit. Today, as I said my final farewell to that dear little person, I was glad I had done it, because she was, unquestionably, the real winner.

> From "Gustie—Gentle, Loving, Determined," *Ask Ann Landers,* April 3, 1973.

Dear Readers: In my 20 years as Ann Landers this is the most difficult column I have ever tried to put together.

I do so after many hours of soul-searching. Should it be written at all? Would it be appropriate? Would it be fair? I have decided yes—because you, my readers, are also my friends. I owe it to you to say something. There should be some word directly from me.

The sad, incredible fact is that after 36 years of marriage Jules and I are being divorced. As I write these words, it is as if I am referring to a letter from a reader. It seems unreal that I am writing about my own marriage.

Many of you may remember the column that appeared in 1969. It was in honor of our 30th wedding anniversary. You may also recall the column I wrote when my beloved mother-in-law, Gustie Lederer, passed away. On both occasions I gave you some intimate glimpses of our life together. Thousands of readers were kind enough to write and say they considered these columns my best.

Every word that appeared in those columns was true when I

wrote them, and very little that was said then could not be said today—in complete honesty.

Jules is an extraordinary man. His nickname for me was "The Queen." He was loving, supportive and generous. He is still all those things—and I will always cherish our wonderful years together.

That we are going our separate ways is one of life's strangest ironies. How did it happen that something so good for so long didn't last forever? The lady with all the answers does not know the answer to this one.

Perhaps there is a lesson there for all of us. At least, it is there for me. "Never say, 'It couldn't happen to us!'"

Please, don't write or call and ask for details. The response would be, "Sorry, this is a personal matter. . . ." Time will not alter my position. I shall continue to say, "No comment." There will be no compromising . . . no exceptions. Just wish us both well.

Not only has this been the most difficult column I ever have written, but also it is the shortest. I apologize to my editors for not giving you your money's worth today. I ask that you not fill this space with other letters. Please leave it blank—as a memorial to one of the world's best marriages that didn't make it to the finish line.

From "A Sad and Personal Message,"
Ask Ann Landers, July 1, 1975.

Edith Cavell

*No one could have been less aptly named than Edith Cavell
(1865–1915), for her name means "happy in war." (Perhaps her
father, an English vicar, and her mother were not aware of this
meaning.) An intelligent and attractive young woman, Edith chose
nursing for her career. For ten years she nursed in England, then
became the Matron of the first teaching hospital in Brussels and
established the Belgian nursing service.*

*When, in 1914, German troops, in order to attack France,
crossed Belgium's frontier, thus violating its neutrality, Edith Cavell watched them enter Brussels. They pushed on and fought the
battle of Mons. Heavily outnumbered, the British Expeditionary
Forces retreated. In the process some soldiers became separated
from their regiments. Two were smuggled into Brussels where Edith
Cavell, as their countrywoman, was asked to shelter them in her
clinic.*

*To her astonishment she suddenly found herself the leader of an
underground escape organization, a role she carried out superbly.
Several hundred Allied soldiers were spirited to safety from her
clinic before her inevitable arrest by the Germans. She spent ten
weeks in prison—for her a time of peace and prayer and reflection—before being shot for treason.*

*Stirling Gahan, who brought Edith Cavell her Last Commu-
nion, was the chaplain at the English church in Brussels. Edith
had been friendly with Gahan and his wife since his appointment
there a year before.*

*A striking statue of Edith Cavell stands around the corner from
the National Art Gallery in London, and only a stone's throw from
Trafalgar Square. On the statue's base are Nurse Cavell's stirring
words to Gahan on his final visit: "Patriotism is not enough. I
must have no hatred or bitterness for anyone."*

Her biographer, Rowland Ryder, writes:

✳ ANOTHER person aware of the situation was the English chaplain, Stirling Gahan. Having vainly tried during the day to get information about Edith Cavell from the Americans, Stirling Gahan returned home to the rue Defacqz at about 6:30 p.m. to find a pencilled note waiting from the German Lutheran Pastor, Paul le Seur: "An English lady, who has not long to live, wishes to see you, and to receive the Holy Communion: come to me at once."

Stirling Gahan had first met Pastor le Seur on July 12, 1915, when he had called upon him in answer to a letter asking for a prayer book for a wounded Englishman: "Found him Christian and courteous," Gahan had noted in his diary. On receiving le Seur's note Gahan went straight to the Pastor's lodging, 18 rue Berlaimont, not knowing to whom the message referred. He arrived at seven o'clock and was shown into le Seur's sitting-room by an orderly. The Pastor arrived—"I thought he was looking rather pale and distressed," wrote Gahan. "To my surprise he opened the conversation by asking me if I knew Nurse Cavell. This was a necessary formality he was bound to observe. I answered, 'Yes, I know her very well, she attends my church, and I have often visited her in her nursing home.' Then he said quietly, 'I am sorry to have to tell you that she has been condemned to death, and is to be shot tomorrow morning.' My feelings at this intelligence I will not attempt to describe. [According to Pastor le Seur, Stirling Gahan almost collapsed on learning of the sentence.] I asked a few questions, and then he proceeded to say, 'I asked her if she would like to receive the Sacrament at your hands, and she said yes. I asked her also if she would like you to be with her at the time of her execution tomorrow morning, but she answered, "No, Mr. Gahan is not used to such things." Then I said, 'I should be quite willing' but Pastor le Seur answered, 'I am very sorry, but it is now too late to obtain that permission.' Then he continued, 'I have here the

permit which will give you admission to St. Gilles prison this evening' " . . .

At 8:30 (9:30 German time) Stirling Gahan arrived with his
Communion set at the prison of St. Gilles; he had braced himself
for the ordeal and prayed for the strength to comfort a fellow
creature who might well be half-demented with shock. "I rung
at the great gate," but he wrote, "and was admitted by a German
warder. He spoke English perfectly, but told me he was a native
of Hamburg. When I informed him whom I had come to visit,
he was at once interested and said, 'She is a fine character,' and
drawing himself up stiffly, said, 'she is like this.' When I asked
how Miss Cavell was, he answered, as if surprised at the question, 'Quite well.' "

It was past 9:30 (German time); Edith Cavell had given up
hope of seeing the Chaplain, but on being told that he had come,
she put on her dressing-gown and was ready in a few moments.
Stirling Gahan wrote an account of how he found her.

"The warder opened the cell door and there stood my friend.
On my way to the prison I had been apprehensive as to the condition of mind in which I might find her. Distraught? Bitter?
Unnerved? Full of hopeless grief? but all anxieties were set at
rest in a moment. There she stood, her bright, gentle, cheerful
self, as always, quietly smiling, calm and collected. She seemed
well in body, quiet in mind and even cheerful and gave me a kind
and grateful welcome."

Edith Cavell smiled, shook hands with Stirling Gahan, ges-
tured to him to sit down on the wooden chair, then—mistress of
meiosis to the last—observed, "It is good of you to come."
Stirling Gahan noticed the forlorn and faded flowers that her
nurses had been allowed to bring her nearly a month before (she
had acknowledged the gift in her letter of September 25). The
cell was clean and sparsely comfortable. They stood for some

time talking. "Miss Cavell said that she expected it would end thus—her trial had been fairly conducted, and her sentence what, under the circumstances, she had expected. She was thankful to God for the absolute quiet of her ten weeks' imprisonment. It had been like a solemn fast from all earthly distractions and diversions."

Some time during this period they sat down, she on the bed and Stirling Gahan on the wooden chair.

"I had no fear nor shrinking," she said. "I have seen death so often that it is not strange or fearful to me . . . life has always been hurried and full of difficulty. This time of rest has been a great mercy. Everyone here has been very kind." Then quietly and clearly she gave her message to the world.

"This I would say, standing as I do in view of God and Eternity, I realize that patriotism is not enough. I must have no hatred or bitterness towards anyone."

"There was no movable table in the cell," wrote Stirling Gahan, "but we sat upon the edge of the bed with the one chair between us. This served as our Communion table, and I placed the vessels, with the bread and wine, upon it. Then we partook of the Lord's Supper together, and she evidently felt deeply the sweet and solemn service. After the Blessing, we remained for a moment silently in prayer, then I began softly to repeat the words of "Abide with Me." At first in a whisper, but soon quite clearly she united with me in the sacred words, and so we repeated together that beautiful hymn of prayer and praise.

"Afterwards she spoke of her sinfulness and unworthiness. How could she be sure that heaven was for her after death? I told the story of the thief on the Cross, with the Saviour's assuring words 'today shalt thou be with me in paradise.' Jesus was almighty to forgive and to save, and to admit all his pardoned ones into his Blessed Presence and Rest. This covered all the need and ended all anxiety."

During the final conversation when she sent farewell messages to friends and relations, Stirling Gahan is reported to have said, "We shall always remember you as a heroine and as a martyr," occasioning the reply, "Don't think of me like that, think of me only as a nurse who tried to do her duty."

Of his last moments with her Gahan wrote: "At length I said, 'Perhaps I had better go now, as you will want to rest.' She gently acquiesced and said, 'Yes, I have to be up at 5:30 a.m.' So we moved to the cell door, and as we stood face to face with a final grasp of our hands, she said sweetly and with a smile, 'We shall meet again.'"

From *Edith Cavell* by Rowland Ryder

Frances Farmer

Frances Farmer (1914–1970) belonged to the Hollywood of the Thirties, the so-called Golden Era of the Silver Screen. She was serious about her career, and progressed from starlet to promising young actress. She was Bing Crosby's leading lady in Rhythm on the Range, *played the coveted dual role in Edna Ferber's* Come and Get It, *was on the cover of* Life. *But something went wrong.*

*For eight years she was an inmate in a state asylum for the insane. During this time she was, she claimed, raped by orderlies, poisoned by tainted food, chained in padded cells, strapped into straitjackets, plunged into icy baths. She emerged, as she records in her autobiography (*Will There Really Be A Morning?*—its innocent title taken from a poem by Emily Dickenson) not vital and victorious but "mutilated, whimpering, and terribly alone."*

She states simply what made it possible for her to get through the devastating years ahead: "I made a friend." The friend was Jean Ratcliffe, a young widow, and her family became Frances Farmer's family as well, the first family she really ever had. Of her Ms. Farmer wrote, "She is the first happy person I have ever met. Life has been gentle to her and she returns it as such."

Two years before Frances Farmer died she became a Catholic. In her final illness her two supports were her friend and her faith.

✳ LIFE took on a new meaning. It was all-powerful. It flowed from me like a wellspring. I was reborn, and I knew that I would have to find a disciplined avenue of faith and worship. Without knowing how, without ever consciously seeking it, God had come into my life, and from that day forth, I began on a path to spiritual fulfillment.

I had changed, and Jean knew it without ever asking how or why. And others knew it. It showed.

I had never given great concern to organized religion, and I was like a wayfaring stranger until one day I found myself sitting in Saint Joan of Arc, the Catholic church of our neighborhood. I had passed the cathedral countless times, but that afternoon, as I was returning from marketing, I stopped and sat alone in the great hall. It was quiet and dark, and I studied the massive altar and understood, for the first time, the power and meaning of the Crucifixion.

I petitioned that very day to begin my instructions and was converted to the Catholic faith. But the conversion was not without personal crucifixion, for the good father who had instructed me suggested that I make my first confession to someone in another church. He wanted me to go where I was a stranger. He was a delightful old man, and I'm sure he pictured me a certain way and preferred to hold to his own thoughts. I went to a downtown church where I was not known, and I have never had such a soul-shattering experience.

I felt it necessary to purge myself in the confessional, but we started off on the wrong foot—he thought I was a man. I have a deep, theatrical voice, my so-called trademark, but to the father, I was someone in the confessional making fun. We finally settled down, and I think I sent him into shock with my confessions. By the time I started counting off the abortions, he was livid and not at all understanding. He reprimanded me so violently I went sobbing from the booth and fell facedown at the altar. I, in his eyes, was an unforgivable sevenfold murderer. My cries brought out the monsignor, who, though puzzled at the commotion, tried to comfort me. I sobbed out my story, and there at the altar that kind and gentle man gave me his blessings.

Horrified by the incident, I wore dark glasses day and night for three weeks. Jean tried to reason that I was starting afresh. She was not of the faith, in fact had no understanding of it, but she realized that unless I was able to face up to and accept the dogmas of my church, of which forgiveness was one, I would be lost in a whirlpool of remorse.

Finally, after days of prayer and petitions, I took off the dark glasses and accepted myself and the world around me.

From the faith I have taken the security that there is a God who loves and directs all things. I have been able to lay aside the grinding hatred and guilts. I still suffer from the past and hope that in time I can better understand the ragged pitfalls into which I have fallen. And yet, if that understanding fails to come, there is a faith now abiding deep within me which promises that I can come through them all unharmed.

I do not choose to proselytize, for I hold strong to the belief that each of us must find our own salvation, and the fact that I did not choose the religion of my closest friends only confirms the freedom of choice and personal discernment that was allowed me. I found my way through their love and understanding, and I elected my faith, though far removed from theirs, of my own free will.

Jean would go to mass with me, and then I would attend her services at Unity, so our Sunday mornings were full of all good things, and though we were far distant in our methods of worship, we were able to bring them together in fellowship and understanding.

And so it was, in 1968, that I laid aside all false appetites. The compulsion to drink the past from my memory faded. The need to obliterate was gone. I was no longer chained. I understood the causes and savored the freedom this understanding brought me. I became positive and solid. My world and my spirit were secure. And my mind was, at last, free.

And I have learned that to have a good friend is the purest of all God's gifts, for it is a love that has no exchange of payment. It is not inherited, as with a family. It is not compelling, as with a child. And it has no means of physical pleasure, as with a mate.

It is, therefore, an indescribable bond that brings with it a far deeper devotion than all the others.

So with gratitude I think of Jean, for she remained when others vanished. She believed when others doubted. And she gave when others received.

Through her, all good was brought into my life, and through the good, I came to know and believe in God.

From *Will There Really Be A Morning?*
by Frances Farmer

Jane Addams

Jane Addams (1860–1935) said her first remembered view of pov-
erty was when she was seven years old. She declared to her father
with much firmness that when she grew up she "should, of course,
have a large house but it would not be built among the other large
houses, but right in the middle of horrid little houses" such as she
was then seeing.

The simple plan which afterwards developed into the Settlement
began to form itself further in her adult mind. Gradually she
became convinced that it would be a good thing to rent a house
in a poor section of the city which could be staffed by well-
educated young women who could learn about life from life itself
as they cared for the needs of the poor. In 1889, with Ellen Gates
Starr, she founded Hull House in Chicago, one of the first social
settlements in the United States, a community center for the neigh-
borhood poor, and also a center for social reform activities. It
exercised influence on the settlement movement throughout the
country.

The hospitable old house which she chose had been originally
the homestead of one of Chicago's pioneer citizens, Charles J.
Hull. Since his time it had passed through many changes includ-
ing, at one time, being used as a furniture store and, at another,
by the Little Sisters of the Poor as a home for the aged.

It was on her initial trip to Europe that Jane Addams saw for
the first time the poor at midnight—a sight she never forgot.

❋ ONE of the most poignant of these experiences, which occurred during the first few months after our landing upon the
other side of the Atlantic, was on a Saturday night, when I received an ineradicable impression of the wretchedness of East
London, and also saw for the first time the over-crowded quarters

of a great city at midnight. A small party of tourists were taken to the East End by a city missionary to witness the Saturday night sale of decaying vegetables and fruit, which, owing to the Sunday laws in London, could not be sold until Monday, and, as they were beyond safe keeping, were disposed of at auction as late as possible on Saturday night. On Mile End Road, from the top of an omnibus which paused at the end of a dingy street lighted by only occasional flares of gas, we saw two huge masses of ill-clad people clamoring around two hucksters' carts. They were bidding their farthings and ha'pennies for a vegetable held up by the auctioneer, which he at last scornfully flung, with a gibe for its cheapness, to the successful bidder. In the momentary pause only one man detached himself from the groups. He had bidden in a cabbage, and when it struck his hand, he instantly sat down on the curb, tore it with his teeth, and hastily devoured it, unwashed and uncooked as it was. He and his fellows were types of the "submerged tenth," as our missionary guide told us, with some little satisfaction in the then new phrase, and he further added that so many of them could scarcely be seen in one spot save at this Saturday night auction, the desire for cheap food being apparently the one thing which could move them simultaneously. They were huddled into ill-fitting, cast-off clothing, the ragged finery which one sees only in East London. Their pale faces were dominated by that most unlovely of human expressions, the cunning and shrewdness of the bargain-hunter who starves if he cannot make a successful trade, and yet the final impression was not of ragged, tawdry clothing nor of pinched and sallow faces, but of myriads of hands, empty, pathetic, nerveless and workworn, showing white in the uncertain light of the street, and clutching forward for food which was already unfit to eat.

Perhaps nothing is so fraught with significance as the human hand, this oldest tool with which man has dug his way from savagery, and with which he is constantly groping forward. I have never since been able to see a number of hands held upward, even when they are moving rhythmically in a calisthenic exercise, or when they belong to a class of chubby children who wave them in eager response to a teacher's query, without a certain revival of this memory, a clutching at the heart reminiscent of the despair and resentment which seized me then.

For the following weeks I went about London almost furtively, afraid to look down narrow streets and alleys lest they disclose again this hideous human need and suffering. I carried with me for days at a time that curious surprise we experience when we first come back into the streets after days given over to sorrow and death; we are bewildered that the world should be going on as usual and unable to determine which is real, the inner pang or the outward seeming. In time all huge London came to seem unreal save the poverty in its East End. During the following two years on the continent, while I was irresistibly drawn to the poorer quarters of each city, nothing among the beggars of South Italy nor among the saltminers of Austria carried with it the same conviction of human wretchedness which was conveyed by this momentary glimpse of an East London street. It was, of course, a most fragmentary and lurid view of the poverty of East London, and quite unfair. I should have been shown either less or more, for I went away with no notion of the hundreds of men and women who had gallantly identified their fortunes with these empty-handed people, and who, in church and chapel, "relief works," and charities, were at least making an effort towards its mitigation.

From *Twenty Years at Hull-House*
by Jane Addams

Zelda Fitzgerald

Saved by being a beauty and the daughter of a respected judge, Zelda Sayre (1900–1948), as she grew up in Montgomery, Alabama, was gossiped about because of her escapades, but not shunned. Her marriage to F. Scott Fitzgerald in 1920 was what one could expect of a witty, intelligent, indulged southern belle. The two moved against a background of glamour supplied by New York, Paris, and the Riviera.

Ten years after their wedding Zelda had the first of the mental breakdowns that were to occur throughout her life. Sadly, some of her most creative work was accomplished while in mental hospitals. It was as a patient that she died in a hospital fire in 1948, eight years after Scott's death.

Just as Zelda was not easy to live with, neither was Scott. Their love was not of the sort that is conducive to mutual strengthening. Nevertheless, their love remained. Scott wrote her during one hospitalization: ". . . the only sadness is living without you, without hearing the notes of your voice. . . . Forget the past . . . and swim back home . . . it is the best refuge for you—turn gently in the waters through which you move and sail back."

Zelda's letters to Scott were also tender and poignant as excerpts below indicate.

❋ ZELDA began to take trips with other patients (rather than in the company of nurses) into Berne and Geneva, and she asked Scott how he could love "a silly girl who buys cheese and plaited bread from enchanted princes in the public market and eats them on the streets. . . ." As her world expanded she tried to let Scott know how delicious her freedom was, as well as how much she missed his presence.

Darling—

I went to Geneva all by myself with a fellow maniac and the city was thick and heavy before the rain . . . . and I wanted to be in Lausanne with you— . . . Have you ever been so lonely that you felt eternally guilty—as if you'd left off part of your clothes—

. . . .

I hope you know there are kisses splattering your balcony to-night from a lady who was once, in three separate letters, a princess in a high white tower,and who has never forgotten her elevated station in life and who is waiting once more for her royal darling

Good-night, honey—

In July there were two idyllic weeks that Zelda spent with Scott and Scottie at Annecy. They said they would "never go there again because those weeks had been perfect and no other time could match them." They played tennis and fished and danced in the warm nights by the lake, "white shoes gleaming like radium in the damp darkness. It was like the good gone times when we still believed in summer hotels and the philosophies of popular songs."

When she was back she teased him playfully, lovingly:

My dearest and most precious Monsieur,

We have here a kind of maniac who seems to have been inspired with erotic aberrations on your behalf. Apart from that she is a person of excellent character, willing to work, would accept a nominal salary while learning, fair complexion, green eyes would like correspondance with refined young man of your description with intent to marry. Previous experience unnecessary. Very fond of family life and a wonderful pet to have in the home. Marked behind the left ear with a slight tendency to schitzoprenie.

Toward the end of the summer Dr. Forel suggested that the Fitzgeralds take another trip together—a trial run so that Zelda might work her way back into society. The Murphys had taken up residence at an old manor house in the Austrian Tyrol; they likened it to a hunting lodge, with its sanded floors and white walls. It was simple and solid and it stood amid beautiful fields of grain. As it was not far from Switzerland, the Fitzgeralds decided to visit them there. Zelda would be with people she liked, she could relax, and the atmosphere was both refreshing and calming. "At first we were petrified at the idea of their coming," Gerald Murphy said. "But once she was there she enjoyed it so, relished it, really. Scott was delighted with the place and enormously reassured by Zelda's behavior." One incident marred the long weekend that the Fitzgeralds spent with them, but it had nothing to do with Zelda. The Murphys had brought with them their nursemaid for their own three children. In the evening when it was time for their baths the nurse asked Scottie (who was nearly ten) if she wanted her bath as well. Scottie rebelled. "She was sure the bathwater was dirty; she thought Mademoiselle had used the same water to bathe each of the three Murphy children. It was cloudy and she ran and told her mother and father. Zelda took it beautifully, but Scott—well, Scott behaved like a child, he made a great deal of fuss over the whole thing." Bath salts, which clouded the water, had been used to soften it, and Scottie thought it was dirty. Scott may also have been more worried than he let on about the tuberculosis of one of the Murphy sons. He had always thought of himself as tubercular and he must have been anxious about Scottie's coming in contact with it. Gerald Murphy said: 'Well, it's all written into *Tender Is the Night*—changed a little of course. But we were stunned, we would never have dreamed of washing them all in the same water!'"

Zelda had passed those various tests of her ability to cope with her life with Scott and her child. She was now able to reassure Scott when he felt blue about their future together.

Please don't be depressed: nothing is sad about you except your sadness and the frayed places on your pink kimona and that you care so much about everything— You are the only person who's ever done all they had to do, damn well, and had enough left over to be dissatisfied. . . . Can't you possibly be just a little bit glad that we are alive and that all the year that's coming we can be to-gether and work and love and get some peace for all the things we've paid 'so much for learning? Stop looking for solace: there isn't any, and if there were life would be a baby affair. . . .

Stop thinking about our marriage and your work and human relations—you are not a showman arranging an exhibit— You are a Sun-god with a wife who loves him and an artist—to take in, assimilate and all alterations to be strictly on paper—

On September 15, 1931, after a year and three months of treatment, Zelda was released from Prangins. Her case was summarized as a "reaction to her feelings of inferiority (primarily toward her husband). . . ." She was stated to have had ambitions which were "self-deceptions" and which "caused difficulties between the couple." Her prognosis was favorable—as long as conflicts could be avoided.

From *Zelda* by Nancy Milford

Emmeline Pankhurst

Emmeline Pankhurst (1858–1928) was a British woman suffragist. Finding little interest for the cause of women's suffrage in the Liberal Party, the Fabian Society, and the Independent Labour Party, all organizations she thought should rally to the cause, she founded (1903) her own movement, the Women's Social and Political Union.

Concerned women in England worked for many painful years to achieve the vote. Mrs. Pankhurst tells of her children even when very young being exposed to the movement. As they grew older they used to talk together about suffrage. One day, her daughter, Christabel, startled her with the remark, "How long you women have been trying for the vote. For my part, I mean to get it."

Much had to be done before it was gotten. Emmeline Pankhurst sparked the first suffrage procession in London. She continually sponsored spectacular, militant means to further the cause, and members of the movement were frequently arrested. Imprisoned in 1912, she went on a hunger strike and was released. This was to be the pattern she followed for more than a dozen imprisonments.

When World War I came she turned her efforts to war work, and at its end went to Canada for several years. She returned to her country in 1926, a nationally revered figure.

The first resolution in favor of female suffrage to be presented to the House of Lords was in 1851 although the movement was older than that. It was not until after the First World War that a limited suffrage was granted women, and not until 1928 that voting rights for women were equalized with those of men.

❋ AT length the opening day of Parliament arrived. On February 19, 1906, occurred the first suffrage procession in London. I think there were between three and four hundred women in that procession, poor working-women from the East End, for the most part, leading the way in which numberless women of every rank were afterward to follow. My eyes were misty with tears as I saw them, standing in line, holding the simple banners which my daughter Sylvia had decorated, waiting for the word of command. Of course our procession attracted a large crowd of intensely amused spectators. The police, however, made no attempt to disperse our ranks, but merely ordered us to furl our banners. There was no reason why we should not have carried banners but the fact was that we were women, and therefore could be bullied. So, bannerless, the procession entered Caxton Hall. To my amazement it was filled with women, most of whom I had never seen at any suffrage gathering before.

Our meeting was most enthusiastic, and while Annie Kenney was speaking, to frequent applause, the news came to me that the King's speech (which is not the King's at all, but the formally announced Government programme for the session) had been read, and that there was in it no mention of the women's suffrage question. As Annie took her seat I arose and made this announcement, and I moved a resolution that the meeting should at once proceed to the House of Commons to urge the members to introduce a suffrage measure. The resolution was carried, and we rushed out in a body and hurried toward the Strangers' Entrance. It was pouring rain and bitterly cold, yet no one turned back, even when we learned at the entrance that for the first time in memory the doors of the House of Commons were barred to women. We sent in our cards to members who were personal friends, and some of them came out and urged our admittance. The police, however, were obdurate. They had their orders. The Liberal government, advocates of the people's rights, had given orders that women should no longer set foot in their stronghold.

Pressure from members proved too great, and the government relented to the extent of allowing twenty women at a time to enter the lobby. Through all the rain and cold those hundreds of women waited for hours their turn to enter. Some never got in, and for those of us who did there was small satisfaction. Not a member could be persuaded to take up our cause.

Out of the disappointment and dejection of that experience I yet reaped a richer harvest of happiness than I had ever known before. Those women had followed me to the House of Commons. They had defied the police. They were awake at last. They were prepared to do something that women had never done before—fight for themselves. Women had always fought for men, and for their children. Now they were ready to fight for their own human rights. Our militant movement was established.

From *My Own Story* by Emmeline Pankhurst

Dolly Madison

Dolly Payne Madison (1763–1849) knew all of the presidents of the United States from George Washington to Zachary Taylor, and she was married to one: James Madison. She was brought up according to the strict principles of Quakerism, and lived by the Book of Discipline until her second marriage.

Through her marriage to Madison she became part of a grand pageant but at heart she remained a simple Quaker. Madison was forty-three when he suggested marriage to Dolly Payne Todd, at twenty-six a widow of almost a year. As soon as they were married, she was introduced to political life, a life that became more and more demanding.

On March 4, 1809, James Madison was inaugurated as President. Dolly Madison soon came to be regarded as the country's first First Lady. Her predecessors had not wished to assume the role of public hostess, a role Mrs. Madison played with ease and grace. The War of 1812, between the United States and Great Britain, imposed upon her yet another role: militant wife.

The British, on August 24, marched into Washington, setting fire to the Capitol. Next they burned the President's House. Once all the government buildings had been burned, President Madison mounted his horse and rode around conducting his official business from his saddle.

Before the President's House was burned, but knowing it might happen at any moment, Dolly Madison wrote to her sister, Lucy Washington Todd.

 Tuesday, August 23, 1814

DEAR SISTER,
    My husband left me yesterday morning to join General Winder.

He inquired anxiously whether I had courage or firmness to remain in the President's house until his return on the morrow, or succeeding day, and on my assurance that I had no fear but for him, and the success of our army, he left, beseeching me to take care of myself, and of the Cabinet papers, public and private. I have since received two despatches from him, written with a pencil. The last is alarming, because he desires I should be ready at a moment's warning to enter my carriage, and leave the city; that the enemy seemed stronger than had at first been reported, and it might happen that they would reach the city with the intention of destroying it. I am accordingly ready; I have pressed as many Cabinet papers into trunks as to fill one carriage; our private property must be sacrificed, as it is impossible to procure wagons for its transportation. I am determined not to go myself until I see Mr. Madison safe, so that he can accompany me, as I hear of much hostility towards him. Dissaffection stalks around us. My friends and acquaintances are all gone, even Colonel C. with his hundred, who were stationed as a guard in this enclosure. French John (a faithful servant), with his usual activity and resolution, offers to spike the cannon at the gate, and lay a train of powder, which would blow up the British, should they enter the house. To the last proposition I positively object, without being able to make him understand why all advantages in war may not be taken.

Wednesday Morning, twelve o'clock.—Since sunrise I have been turning my spy-glass in every direction, and watching with unwearied anxiety, hoping to discover the approach of my dear husband and his friends; but, alas! I can descry only groups of military, wandering in all directions, as if there was a lack of arms, or of spirit to fight for their own fireside.

Three o'clock.—Will you believe it, my sister? We have a battle, or skirmish, near Bladensburg, and here I am still, within sound of the cannon! Mr. Madison comes not. May God protect us! Two messengers, covered with dust, come to bid me fly; but here I mean to wait for him . . . At this late hour a wagon has been procured, and I have had it filled with plate and the most valuable portable articles, belonging to the house. Whether it will reach its destination, the "Bank of Maryland," or fall into the hands of British soldiery, events must determine. Our kind friend, Mr. Carroll, has come to hasten my departure, and in a very bad humor with me, because I insist on waiting until the large picture of General Washington is secured, and it requires to be unscrewed from the wall. This process was found too tedious for these perilous moments; I have ordered the frame to be broken, and the canvas taken out. It is done! and the precious portrait placed in the hands of two gentlemen of New York, for safe keeping. And now, dear sister, I must leave this house, or the retreating army will make me a prisoner in it by filling up the road I am directed to take. When I shall again write to you, or where I shall be tomorrow, I cannot tell!

Dolly

From *Memoirs and Letters of Dolly Madison*, edited by her grand-niece

Marian Anderson

Marian Anderson (1902–   ) was the first black person to be named a permanent member of the Metropolitan Opera Company and she recalls it as a highlight of her life. Her first great successes, however, were in Europe. A contralto, her rich, wide-ranged voice was magnificently suited to both opera and Negro spirituals. (Of these latter the most precious to her is "He Has the Whole World in His Hands.") After putting herself under Sol Hurok's management she began singing more in this country than in Europe.

Hurok arranged a concert for Marian Anderson in Constitution Hall in 1939. In a decision that shook the country, the Daughters of the American Revolution, owners of the hall, announced they would not permit it to be used by a black. Eleanor Roosevelt, then the First Lady, resigned her DAR membership, and sponsored Marian Anderson's concert at the Lincoln Memorial on Easter Sunday.

Belatedly, in 1943, Marian Anderson sang for the first time in Constitution Hall. That night I was a member of the audience which had a quiet sense of history in the making. But no triumphalism marred the evening. It was a moving and beautiful concert by a great artist. The magic performance which she describes here had taken place a few years earlier on Easter Sunday at the Lincoln Memorial.

❋ THE excitement over the denial of Constitution Hall to me did not die down. It seemed to increase and to follow me wherever I went. I felt about the affair as about an election campaign; whatever the outcome, there is bound to be unpleasantness and embarrassment. I could not escape it, of course. My friends wanted to discuss it, and even strangers went out of their way to express their strong feelings of sympathy and support.

What were my own feelings? I was saddened and ashamed. I was sorry for the people who had precipitated the affair. I felt that their behavior stemmed from a lack of understanding. They were not persecuting me personally or as a representative of my people so much as they were doing something that was neither sensible nor good. Could I have erased the bitteness, I would have done so gladly. I do not mean that I would have been prepared to say that I was not entitled to appear in Constitution Hall as might any other performer. But the unpleasantness disturbed me, and if it had been up to me alone I would have sought a way to wipe it out. I cannot say that such a way out suggested itself to me at the time, or that I thought of one after the event. But I have been in this world long enough to know that there are all kinds of people, all suited by their own natures for different tasks. It would be fooling myself to think that I was meant to be a fearless fighter; I was not, just as I was not meant to be a soprano instead of a contralto.

Then the time came when it was decided that I would sing in Washington on Easter Sunday. The invitation to appear in the open, singing from the Lincoln Memorial before as many people as would care to come, without charge, was made formally by Harold L. Ickes, Secretary of the Interior. It was duly reported, and the weight of the Washington affair bore in on me.

Easter Sunday in 1939 was April 9, and I had other concert dates to fill before it came. Wherever we went I was met by reporters and photographers. The inevitable question was, "What about Washington?" My answer was that I knew too little to tell an intelligent story about it. There were occasions, of course, when I knew more than I said. I did not want to talk, and I particularly did not want to say anything about the D.A.R. As I have made clear, I did not feel that I was designed for hand-to-hand combat, and I did not wish to make statements that I would later regret. The management was taking action. That was enough.

It was comforting to have concrete expressions of support for an essential principle. It was touching to hear from a local manager in a Texas city that a block of two hundred tickets had been purchased by the community's D.A.R. people. It was also heartening; it confirmed my conviction that a whole group should not be condemned because an individual or section of the group does a thing that is not right.

I was informed of the plan for the outdoor concert before the news was published. Indeed, I was asked whether I approved. I said yes, but the yes did not come easily or quickly. I don't like a lot of show, and one could not tell in advance what direction the affair would take. I studied my conscience. In principle the idea was sound, but it could not be comfortable to me as an individual. As I thought further, I could see that my significance as an individual was small in this affair. I had become, whether I liked it or not, a symbol, representing my people. I had to appear.

I discussed the problem with Mother, of course. Her comment was characteristic: "It is an important decision to make. You are in this work. You intend to stay in it. You know what your aspirations are. I think you should make your own decision."

Mother knew what the decision would be. In my heart I also knew. I could not run away from this situation. If I had anything to offer, I would have to do so now. It would be misleading, however, to say that once the decision was made I was without doubts.

We reached Washington early that Easter morning and went to the home of Gifford Pinchot, who had been Governor of Pennsylvania. The Pinchots had been kind enough to offer their hospitality, and it was needed because the hotels would not take us. Then we drove over to the Lincoln Memorial. Kosti was well enough to play, and we tried out the piano and examined the public-address system, which had six microphones, meant not only for the people who were present but also for a radio audience.

When we returned that afternoon I had sensations unlike any I had experienced before. The only comparable emotion I could recall was the feeling I had had when Maestro Toscanini had appeared in the artist's room in Salzburg. My heart leaped wildly, and I could not talk. I even wondered whether I would be able to sing.

The murmur of the vast assemblage quickened my pulse beat. There were policemen waiting at the car, and they led us through a passageway that other officers kept open in the throng. We entered the monument and were taken to a small room. We were introduced to Mr. Ickes, whom we had not met before. He outlined the program. Then came the signal to go out before the public.

If I did not consult contemporary reports I could not recall who was there. My head and heart were in such turmoil that I looked and hardly saw, I listened and hardly heard. I was led to the platform by Representative Caroline O'Day of New York, who had been born in Georgia, and Oscar Chapman, Assistant Secretary of the Interior, who was a Virginian. On the platform behind me sat Secretary Ickes, Secretary of the Treasury Morgenthau, Supreme Court Justice Black, Senators Wagner, Mead, Barkley, Clark, Guffey, and Capper, and many Representatives, including Representative Arthur W. Mitchell of Illinois, a Negro. Mother was there as were people from Howard University and from churches in Washington and other cities. So was Walter White, then secretary of the National Association for the Advancement of Colored People. It was Mr. White who at one point stepped to the microphone and appealed to the crowd, probably averting serious accidents when my own people tried to reach me.

I report these things now because I have looked them up. All I knew then as I stepped forward was the overwhelming impact of that vast multitude. There seemed to be people as far as the eye could see. The crowd stretched in a great semi-circle from the Lincoln Memorial around the reflecting pool on to the shaft of the Washington Monument. I had a feeling that a great wave of good will poured out from these people, almost engulfing me. And when I stood up to sing our National Anthem I felt for a moment as though I were choking. For a desperate second I thought that the words, well as I know them, would not come.

I sang, I don't know how. There must have been the help of professionalism I had accumulated over the years. Without it I could not have gone through the program. I sang—and again I know because I consulted a newspaper clipping—"America," the aria "O mio Fernando," Schubert's "Ave Maria," and three spirituals—"Gospel Train," "Trampin'," and "My Soul is Anchored in the Lord."

I regret that a fixed rule was broken, another thing about which I found out later. Photographs were taken from within the Memorial, where the great statue of Lincoln stands, although there was a tradition that no pictures could be taken from within the sanctum.

It seems also that at the end, when the tumult of the crowd's shouting would not die down, I spoke a few words. I read the clipping now and cannot believe that I could have uttered another sound after I had finished singing. "I am overwhelmed," I said. "I just can't talk. I can't tell you what you have done for me today. I thank you from the bottom of my heart again and again."

It was the simple truth. But did I really say it?

There were many in the gathering who were stirred by their own emotions. Perhaps I did not grasp all that was happening, but at the end great numbers of people bore down on me. They were friendly; all they wished to do was to offer their congratulations and good wishes. The police felt that such a concentration of people was a danger, and they escorted me back into the Memorial. Finally we returned to the Pinchot home.

I cannot forget that demonstration of public emotion or my own strong feelings. In the years that have passed I have had constant reminders of that Easter Sunday. It is not at all uncommon to have people come backstage after a concert even now and remark, "You know, I was at that Easter concert." In my travels abroad I have met countless people who heard and remembered about that Easter Sunday.

From *My Lord, What a Morning* by Marian Anderson

Anne Morrow Lindbergh

Anne Morrow Lindbergh, (1906–   ), is a gallant, sensitive, intelligent woman. Her marriage, in 1929, to Charles Lindbergh brought together two remarkable persons, deserving of each other. After their marriage she accompanied him on his survey flights and later reported on these trips in books combining careful information with imaginative prose. Her adult life has been many-faceted, reflecting her devotion to her home and family (five children) as well as to aviation and to a distinguished literary career.

Success in all of these areas has called for a wise management of time. Anne Morrow Lindbergh in Gift from the Sea *indicates how an ideal, single day should be spent. "Evening is the time for conversation. Morning is for mental work, I felt, the habit of school-days persisting in me. Afternoon is for physical tasks, the out-of-door jobs. But evening is for sharing, for communication. Is it the uninterrupted dark expanse of the night after the bright segmented day, that frees us to each other? Or does the infinite space and infinite darkness dwarf and chill us, turning us to seek small human sparks?"*

Not all her days have been thus spent. Nor have all her days been happy days. Her sorrow has gone beyond that normally borne by us all. The Lindberghs' infant son (and first child) was kidnapped from their home in Hopewell, New Jersey, on March 1, 1932. The demanded ransom of $50,000 was paid but the baby was not returned, and in May his battered corpse was found near Hopewell.

There possibly has never been a personal tragedy that the country has identified with more totally—and this before the medium of television. The nation's grief could, however, only be a reflection of the Lindberghs' grief. In her diary Anne Morrow Lindbergh gave poignant expression to that grief.

❋   Monday, January 30, 1933
Terrible night. "Do you think about it so much, Anne?" All the
time—it never stops—I never meet it. It happens every night—
every night of my life. *It did not happen* and *It happened.* For I
go over the possibilities of its not happening—so close, so narrow
they are. So hard do I think about it that almost I make it un-
happen. That terrible feeling, that pushing against a stone wall,
that insisting "No, it didn't happen, it didn't happen"—and then
always, like a bell tolling, like a clock striking, inevitable: "It
happened." Then, at last, back to the only comfort—Death: We
will all have it. In a century this distance between him and me
will be nothing.

And then: He did not suffer, he did not know, a blow on the
head.

But I want to know—to know just what he suffered—I want
to see it, to feel it even.

                                          Wednesday, February 1, 1933
My last month of him—and the shortest one of the year.

                                             Sunday, February 5, 1933
To Hopewell. I make an excuse of it to ask C. questions; weak
of me. "I went through it last spring—I can't go through it
again."

There is the difference between men and women. I never went
through it really then. I never accepted it. I never experienced it
and I will *never* be through with it. I feel sometimes frantic,
battling against time—this strange time that I thought marched
along in orderly fashion to the tick of the clock. And now it does
not move, it stays frozen inside of me.

                                          Thursday, February 16, 1933
It isn't the sorrow of last winter that stabs, it is those moments
of hope—remembering those moments of hope is unbearable.

I planned to have him sleep in my bed the first night he came back.

It is not hard looking back at sorrow but at happiness.

And oh Jon! I walked into his room and he lifted his sleek soft head from the bed and looked up at me with his big wide eyes and then just smiled quietly, as if to say, "You back again? Oh, yes. . . ." He looked strangely like little Charles, perhaps because he looks more of a real person, bigger. I've had him all day today. I came in early this morning and he was lying on his back with a lump in the bedclothes where he was pushing up his feet, and he was playing intently with your white wool rabbit. He smiled that quiet unsurprised-secret-understanding smile of a child—like little Charles again—when he saw me.

I was very happy today. It was a beautiful day, like spring; there were red and green points of tulips coming up and the maples look red. I walked through the woods and sat on a log in the sun. I realized that I hadn't felt that way for a long time, relieved of some great pain and heaviness. Wanting to live, and believing things were good, as though with the spring I could shake off the terrible winter preoccupation with the crime and think of little Charles as belonging to spring—as he did that day, the spring before, when I wheeled him over the brook and we sat in the sunshine and I thought, "This is pure joy—nothing else matters." As if spring could bring back that essence. I felt a wonderful stream flowing through me that was this life—all this eternal life—going on, and it was joyful.

From *Locked Rooms and Open Doors*
by Anne Morrow Lindbergh

Virginia Woolf

Virginia Stephen Woolf (1882–1941), English novelist and essayist, was sharp of mind and sharp of tongue. She was also a woman of beauty. Her sister, Vanessa, said, "She reminded me always of a sweet pea of a special flame colour."

Life for Virginia Woolf seemed always to be marked by intensity, both glorious and tragic. Early horrifying nursery experiences with her half-brother appear to have left her with a deep aversion to sex. Quentin Bell, her biographer and nephew, suggests that she "regarded sex not so much with horror as with incomprehension." Her first breakdown came when she was thirteen. As Bell sadly points out, "From now on she knew that she had been mad and might be mad again."

In 1911, Leonard Woolf fell very deeply in love with her. In a letter to her after he had proposed, he wrote, "I am selfish, jealous, cruel, lustful, a liar, and probably worse still. I had said over and over again to myself that I would never marry anyone because of this, mostly because I think I felt I could never control these things with a woman who was inferior and would gradually enfuriate me by her inferiority and submission . . . It is because you aren't that that risk is so infinitely less."

A little over a year and a half later they were married. Of them Bell wrote, "Their love and admiration for each other, based as it was upon a real understanding of the good qualities in each, was strong enough to withstand the major and minor punishments of fortune, the common vexations of matrimony and, presently, the horrors of madness. It is a proof of their deep and unvarying affection that it was not dependent upon the intense joys of physical love."

And when in 1941, Virginia Woolf, plagued yet again by approaching madness, took her life by drowning, she wrote to her husband, "Dearest, I want to tell you that you have given me complete happiness."

A critic once said of Virginia Woolf's work that "The subject of her writing was the little world of people like herself, a small class, a dying class, . . . a class with inherited privileges, private incomes, sheltered lives, protected sensibilities, sensitive tastes. Outside of this class she knows very little."

This essay on Mrs. Grey and old age goes well beyond that "little world."

✻ THERE are moments even in England, now, when even the busiest, most contented suddenly let fall what they hold—it may be the week's washing. Sheets and pyjamas crumble and dissolve in their hands, because, though they do not state this in so many words, it seems silly to take the washing round to Mrs. Peel when out there over the fields over the hills, there is no washing; no pinning of clothes-lines; mangling and ironing; no work at all, but boundless rest. Stainless and boundless rest; space un-limited; untrodden grass; wild birds flying; hills whose smooth uprise continues that wild flight.

Of all this however only seven foot by four could be seen from Mrs. Grey's corner. That was the size of her front door which stood wide open, though there was a fire burning in the grate. The fire looked like a small spot of dusty light feebly trying to escape from the embarrassing pressure of the pouring sunshine.

Mrs. Grey sat on a hard chair in the corner looking—but at what? Apparently at nothing. She did not change the focus of her eyes when visitors came in. Her eyes had ceased to focus them-selves; it may be that they had lost the power. They were aged eyes, blue, unspectacled. They could see, but without looking. She had never used her eyes on anything minute and difficult; merely upon faces, and dishes and fields. And now at the age of ninety-two they saw nothing but a zigzag of pain wriggling across the door, pain that twisted her legs as it wriggled; jerked her body to and fro like a marionette. Her body was wrapped round the pain as a damp sheet is folded over a wire. The wire was spasmodically jerked by a cruel invisible hand. She flung out a foot, a hand. Then it stopped. She sat still for a moment.

In that pause she saw herself in the past at ten, at twenty, at twenty-five. She was running in and out of a cottage with eleven brothers and sisters. The line jerked. She was thrown forward in her chair.

"All dead. All dead," she mumbled. "My brothers and sisters. And my husband gone. My daughter too. But I go on. Every morning I pray God to let me pass."

The morning spread seven foot by four green and sunny. Like a fling of grain the birds settled on the land. She was jerked again by another tweak of the tormenting hand.

"I'm an ignorant old woman. I can't read or write, and every morning when I crawls downstairs, I say I wish it were night; and every night, when I crawls up to bed, I say I wish it were day. I'm only an ignorant old woman. But I prays to God: O let me pass. I'm an ignorant old woman—I can't read or write."

So when the colour went out of the doorway, she could not see the other page which is then lit up; or hear the voices that have argued, sung, talked for hundreds of years.

The jerked limbs were still again.

"The doctor comes every week. The parish doctor now. Since my daughter went, we can't afford Dr. Nicholls. But he's a good man. He says he wonders I don't go. He says my heart's nothing but wind and water. Yet I don't seem able to die."

So we—humanity—insist that the body shall still cling to the wire. We put out the eyes and the ears; but we pinion it there, with a bottle of medicine, a cup of tea, a dying fire, like a rook on a barn door; but a rook that still lives, even with a nail through it.

From "Old Mrs. Grey," *Collected Essays*
by Virginia Woolf

Ellen Terry

As a member of a famous English theatrical family, Ellen Terry (1848–1928) made her debut on the stage at the age of eight, and played juvenile roles until she was sixteen. For six years she was away from the stage (long enough to marry unhappily one man and to have two children by another).

An actress of charm, beauty, and joyousness, she became Sir Henry Irving's leading lady, acting with him in this country as well as in England. They have been acclaimed as "the greatest partnership in the history of the English theatre," although he was the actor of genius and she, according to her own analysis, "more woman than artist." Yet she was highly talented, and always wanted to make the best use of her gifts on stage, even though she was not possessed by Irving's devouring genius.

She had a long correspondence with Bernard Shaw, begun when he was almost thirty-six and she was forty-five. Shaw called his correspondence with her "a paper courtship," and regarded it as "perhaps the pleasantest, as it is the most enduring of all courtships." Of her at the height of her power he wrote, "Ellen Terry is the most beautiful name in the world; it rings like a chime through the last quarter of the nineteenth century."

She acted until she was past her mid-seventies. Her final role was in Walter de la Mare's play Crossings *in 1925.*

❋ IT was Mrs. Kean who chose me out of five or six other children to play my first part. We were all tried in it, and when we had finished, she said the same thing to us all:

"That's very nice! Thank you, my dear. That will do."

We none of us knew at the time which of us had pleased her most.

At this time we were living in the upper part of a house in the

Gower Street region. That first home in London I remember chiefly by its fine brass knocker, which mother kept beautifully bright, and by its being the place to which was sent my first part! Bound in green American cloth, it looked to me more marvellous than the most priceless book has ever looked since! I was so proud and pleased and delighted that I danced a hornpipe for joy!

Why was I chosen, and not one of the other children, for the part of Mamilius? some one may ask. It was not mere luck, I think. Perhaps I was a born actress, but that would have served me little if I had not been able to *speak!* It must be remembered that both my sister Kate and I had been trained almost from our birth for the stage, and particularly in the important branch of clear articulation. Father, as I have already said, was a very charming elocutionist, and my mother read Shakespeare beautifully. They were both very fond of us and saw our faults with the eyes of love, though they were unsparing in their corrections. In these early days they had need of all their patience, for I was a most troublesome, wayward pupil. However, "the labour we delight in physics pain," and I hope, too, that my more staid sister made it up to them!

The rehearsals for "A Winter's Tale" were a lesson in fortitude. They taught me once and for all that an actress's life (even when the actress is only eight) is not all beer and skittles, or cakes and ale, or fame and glory. I was cast for the part of Mamilius in the way I have described, and my heart swelled with pride when I was told what I had to do, when I realized that I had a real Shakespeare part—a possession that father had taught me to consider the pride of life!

But many weary hours were to pass before the first night. If a company has to rehearse four hours a day now, it is considered a great hardship, and players must lunch and dine like other folk. But this was not Kean's way! Rehearsals lasted all day, Sundays included, and when there was no play running at night, until four or five the next morning! I don't think any actor in those days dreamed of luncheon. (Tennyson, by the way, told me to say "luncheon"—not "lunch.") How my poor little legs used to ache! Sometimes I could hardly keep my eyes open when I was on the stage, and often when my scene was over, I used to creep into the greenroom and forget my troubles and my art (if you can talk of art in connection with a child of eight) in a delicious sleep.

At the dress-rehearsals I did not want to sleep. All the members of the company were allowed to sit and watch the scenes in which they were not concerned, from the back of the dress-circle. This, by the way, is an excellent plan, and in theatres where it is followed the young actress has reason to be grateful. In these days of greater publicity when the press attend rehearsals, there may be strong reasons against the company being "in front," but the perfect loyalty of all concerned would dispose of these reasons. Now, for the first time, the beginner is able to see the effect of the weeks of thought and labour which have been given to the production. She can watch from the front the fulfillment of what she has only seen as intention and promise during the other rehearsals. But I am afraid that beginners now are not so keen as they used to be. The first wicked thing I did in a theatre sprang from excess of keenness. I borrowed a knife from a carpenter and made a slit in the canvas to watch Mrs. Kean as Hermione!

Devoted to her art, conscientious to a degree in mastering the spirit and details of her part, Mrs. Kean also possessed the personality and force to chain the attention and indelibly imprint her rendering of a part on the imagination. When I think of the costume in which she played Hermione, it seems marvellous to me that she could have produced the impression that she did. This seems to contradict what I have said about the magnificence of the production. But not at all! The designs of the dresses were purely classic; but then, as now, actors and actresses seemed unable to keep their own period and their own individuality out of the clothes directly they got them on their backs. In some cases the original design was quite swamped. No matter what the character that Mrs. Kean was assuming, she always used to wear her hair drawn flat over her forehead and twisted tight round her ears in a kind of circular sweep—such as the old writing-masters used to make when they attempted an extra grand flourish. And then the amount of petticoats she wore! Even as Hermione she was always bunched out by layer upon layer of petticoats, in defiance of the fact that classical parts should not be dressed in a superfluity of raiment. But if the petticoats were full of starch, the voice was full of pathos—and the dignity, simplicity, and womanliness of Mrs. Charles Kean's Hermione could not have been marred by a far more grotesque costume.

There is something, I suppose, in a woman's nature which always makes her remember how she was dressed at any specially eventful moment of her life, and I can see myself, as though it were yesterday, in the little red-and-silver dress I wore as Mamilius. Mrs. Grieve, the dresser—"Peter Grieve-us," as we children called her—had pulled me into my very pink tights (they were by no means *tight* but very baggy, according to the pictures of me), and my mother had arranged my hair in sausage curls on each side of my head in even more perfect order and regularity than usual. Besides my clothes, I had a beautiful "property" to be proud of. This was a go-cart, which had been made in the theatre by Mr. Bradshaw, and was an exact copy of a child's toy as depicted on a Greek vase. It was my duty to drag this little cart about the stage, and on the first night, when Mr. Kean as Leontes told me to "go play," I obeyed his instructions with such vigour that I tripped over the handle and came down on my back! A titter ran through the house, and I felt that my career as an actress was ruined forever. Even now I remember how bitterly I wept, and how deeply humiliated I felt. But the little incident, so mortifying to me, did not spoil my first appearance altogether. *The Times* of May 1, 1856, was kind enough to call me "vivacious and precocious," and "a worthy relative of my sister Kate," and my parents were pleased (although they would not show it too much), and Mrs. Kean gave me a pat on the back. Father and Kate were both in the cast, too, I ought to have said, and the Queen, Prince Albert, and the Princess Royal were all in a box on the first night.

To act for the first time in Shakespeare, in a theatre where my sister had already done something for our name, and before royalty, was surely a good beginning! From April 28, 1856, I played Mamilius every night for one hundred and two nights. I was never ill, and my understudy, Clara Denvil, a very handsome, dark child with flaming eyes, though quite ready and longing to play my part, never had the chance.

I had now taken the first step, but I had taken it without any notion of what I was doing. I was innocent of all art, and while I loved the actual doing of my part, I hated the labour that led up to it. But the time was soon to come when I was to be fired by a passion for work. Meanwhile I was unconsciously learning a number of lessons which were to be most useful to me in my subsequent career.

*   *   *

Stage fright is like nothing else in the world. You are standing on the stage apparently quite well and in your right mind, when suddenly you feel as if your tongue had been dislocated and was lying powerless in your mouth. Cold shivers begin to creep downwards from the nape of your neck and all up you at the same time, until they seem to meet in the small of your back. About this time you feel as if a centipede, all of whose feet have been carefully iced, has begun to run about in the roots of your hair. The next agreeable sensation is the breaking out of a cold sweat all over. Then you are certain that some one has cut the muscles at the back of your knees. Your mouth begins to open slowly, without giving utterance to a single sound, and your eyes seem inclined to jump out of your head over the footlights. At this point it is as well to get off the stage as quickly as you can, for you are far beyond human help.

Whether everybody suffers in this way or not I cannot say, but it exactly describes the torture I went through in "The Governor's Wife." I had just enough strength and sense to drag myself off the stage and seize a book, with which, after a few minutes, I reappeared and ignominiously read my part. Whether Madame de Rhona boxed my ears or not, I can't remember, but I think it is very likely she did, for she was very quick-tempered. In later years I have not suffered from the fearsome malady, but even now, after fifty years of stage-life, I never play a new part without being overcome by a terrible nervousness and a torturing dread of forgetting my lines. Every nerve in my body seems to be dancing an independent jig on its own account.

From *The Story of My Life* by Ellen Terry

Jory Graham

Jory Graham (1923–   ) was once described by a fellow columnist as "a blend of relaxed chic and quick wit . . . the kind of woman who begins to blossom at 30 and others envy. . . . She is a windblown personality with every hair in place." This comment was made not many months after the publication (1969) of Ms. Graham's book, Chicago: An Extraordinary Guide.

The book had taken two years to write and Ms. Graham, with a trio of young assistants, gridded the city to gather material. Jory Graham knows her city. She is a fourth-generation Chicagoan who grew up (as did Loeb, Leopold, and Bobby Frank) in Kenwood, a charming, old section of Chicago. She attended the University of Chicago in adjacent Hyde Park. After a broken marriage and eleven years of advertising in New York and Chicago she began freelance writing in her native city.

She became a columnist for the Chicago Sun-Times, *writing a weekly column, "Jory Graham's City". In the Seventies, although still a* Sun-Times *columnist, she took a new theme. Her new bi-weekly column was being written "for all of those who must live with the threat of death, either their own or someone near to them." Again, as she had with her book on Chicago, Ms. Graham was writing from first-hand experience: she had cancer which had metastasized.*

Some time after this new series had begun, friends invited Ms. Graham and me for dinner. I arrived first and I can still see her when she came into the room: quick, intense, smartly dressed, balancing lightly on a slim, black cane. When we were introduced I found myself asking, "Do people sometimes feel awkward meeting you?" She answered yes.

She and I were the only guests and during dinner the conversation turned to her column. Jory Graham is the kind of person with whom one quickly gets down to basics. She said she was eager to win occupational acceptance for those ill with cancer. She said, too, she wanted to see legislation that would legalize the drugs that could ease the effects of certain cancer therapy but at that time could only be purchased illegally on the street.

I was hypnotized by her conversation, so much so that a question spilled out almost without my realizing. I asked her if she believed in eternity. She answered decisively, "I believe in Living."

✳ I GREW up in a medical atmosphere at a time when cancer patients were almost never told the truth about their illness. Even when they guessed, they were given euphemisms—"It's just a complicated obstruction"—or whatever. The entire medical profession, my father included, apparently was tacitly engaged in a vast conspiracy urged on by families: "We must not let the poor devil know."

That background left me somewhat paranoid about doctors. When I was old enough to choose my own, I shopped endlessly for one who would not play God with my body and my life. If something is critically wrong with my body, I want to know about it. And if what is wrong will affect the rest of my life, I have the right to know that, too.

A sparkling cocktail party last Christmas was nearly ruined for me because of a quiet-corner discussion with an eminent cancer specialist. I knew him, respected him, had interviewed him. We drifted into a discussion on cancer and I suddenly heard him say that if the spouse or the family of a cancer patient asked him to hide the fact of cancer from the patient, he would honor the request.

"What about the patient?" I asked. "Mightn't that be disrespectful of his wishes, and the fact that he might want the truth?"

"I am just old-fashioned enough," the cancer specialist said, "to believe that families know best."

"That's a copout," I said as politely as I could. And then, because I'm old-fashioned enough to believe that guests at a party have an obligation not to get into screaming arguments, I excused myself. I was angry and disillusioned—another great man playing God.

What a pity that our medical histories taken by physicians do not include a stock question: "If, at some future date, we diagnose a possibly fatal illness, would you want to know?" This would eliminate confusion and guilt as to who plays God with whom.

In January, my own physicians quietly told me that cancer had metastisized to my spine. Despite my terror then and the fear that still haunts me now, I am ahead because I have not been conned.

To be conned about a fatal disease is an even greater tragedy than the disease itself. It is to be cheated of the basic human right to make decisions about the time that is still yours. When others decide that you must not know what your illness is, they enter into a terrible game. Don't-let-on not only puts insane constraints on the players but robs them—and the one they believe they are protecting—of the chance to share any longer anything worthwhile.

Because I can be candid about a recurrence of cancer, I make day-to-day living easier for myself and those around me. If I am in pain, I can say so and can then go on working with colleagues or sharing dinner with friends.

As for those I am closest to, love shared under present circumstances is love such as I have never known until now. The limitation of our time together makes more poignant and valuable the good things we still share.

Had my doctors been less candid with me, all this would have been denied me. To deny it to others in the name of God-knows-what motive is to negate closeness, intimacy and the magnitude of love.

> From the column "What About the Patient and His Right to Know?" by Jory Graham.
> *Chicago Daily News,* July 4, 1977

Queen Victoria

Although Victoria (1819–1901) was the child of the Duke of Kent, (the fourth son of George III), even before her birth it was expected that she would ascend the English throne. At her birth she was described as "a pretty little Princess, as plump as a partridge." Plump as a partridge she was often to look in pictures the rest of her life.

Before she was a year old, her father died, and her upbringing under her mother, the Duchess of Kent, became strained and unnatural even for a princess. Her mother, in turn, was under the influence of John Conroy, devouringly ambitious and without scruple. These two attempted to bring up Victoria totally dependent upon her mother so that if she became queen before she was eighteen, as seemed possible, there would have to be a regency, and this would be controlled by the Duchess of Kent. As much as possible she was kept separated from other members of the Royal Family. Very much alone, at the same time she was never allowed by her mother an opportunity to be really alone. For playmates she had only the Conroy daughters, whom she detested—as she did their father.

Only a remarkably strong psyche could survive and Victoria managed. There were, of course, times of joy. Very occasional visits, but frequent letters from her mother's brother, King Leopold I of Belgium and Queen Louise and from her half-sister, Princess Feodora, all people she deeply loved. In addition, she had the helpful presence of her "sub-governess," Baroness Lehzen, a strong woman who refused to be influenced by the Duchess and Conroy.

Contrary to the hopes of the Duchess and Conroy, Victoria did not succeed to the throne until she was eighteen. In the weeks before King William's imminent death the Duchess and Conroy daily launched violent attacks upon her to secure a promise to put Conroy at the head of all her affairs when she came to the throne. It is questionable how much longer she could have withstood such pressure had the King not died.

In her journal she described receiving the official word of his death and her accession. In the light of her early life one understands more fully her repeated use of the word "alone" in the journal entry.

✳   Tuesday, 20th June 1837

I WAS awoke at 6 o'clock by Mamma, who told me that the Archbishop of Canterbury and Lord Conyngham were here, and wished to see me. I got out of bed and went into my sitting-room (only in my dressing-gown) and *alone,* and saw them. Lord Conyngham (the Lord Chamberlain) then acquainted me that my poor Uncle, the King, was no more, and had expired at 12 minutes past 2 this morning, and consequently that I am *Queen.* Lord Conyngham knelt down and kissed my hand, at the same time delivering to me the official announcement of the poor King's demise. The Archbishop then told me that the Queen was desirous that he should come and tell me the details of the last moments of my poor good Uncle; he said that he had directed his mind to religion, and had died in a perfectly happy, quiet state of mind, and was quite prepared for his death. He added that the King's sufferings at the last were not very great but that there was a good deal of uneasiness. Lord Conyngham, whom I charged to express my feelings of condolence and sorrow to the poor Queen, returned directly to Windsor. I then went to my room and dressed.

Since it has pleased Providence to place me in this station, I shall do my utmost to fulfil my duty towards my country; I am very young and perhaps in many, though not in all things, inexperienced, but I am sure that very few have more real goodwill and more real desire to do what is fit and right than I have.

Breakfasted, during which time good, faithful Stockmar came and talked to me. Wrote a letter to dear Uncle Leopold and a few words to dear good Feodore. Received a letter from Lord Melbourne in which he said he would wait upon me at a little before 9. At 9 came Lord Melbourne, whom I saw in my room, and of *course quite alone,* as I shall *always* do all my Ministers. He kissed my hand, and I then acquainted him that it had long been my intention to retain him and the rest of the present Ministry at the head of affairs, and that it could not be in better hands than his. He again then kissed my hand. He then read to me the Declaration which I was to read to the Council, which he wrote himself, and which is a very fine one. I then talked with him some little time longer, after which he left me. He was in full dress. I like him very much and feel confidence in him. He is a very straightforward, honest, clever and good man. I then wrote a letter to the Queen. At about 11 Lord Melbourne came again to me, and spoke to me upon various subjects. At about half-past 11 I went downtstairs and held a Council in the red saloon.

I went in of course quite alone and remained seated the whole time. My two Uncles, the Dukes of Cumberland and Sussex, and Lord Melbourne conducted me. The Declaration, the various forms, the swearing in of the Privy Councillors of which there were a great number present, and the reception of some of the Lords of the Council, previous to the Council, in an adjacent room (likewise alone) I subjoin here. I was not at all nervous and had the satisfaction of hearing that people were satisfied with what I had done and how I had done it. Received after this, audiences of Lord Melbourne, Lord John Russell, Lord Albemarle (Master of the Horse), and the Archbishop of Canterbury, all in my room and alone. Saw Stockmar. Saw Clark, whom I named my Physician. Saw Mary. Wrote to Uncle Ernest. Saw Ernest Hohenlohe, who brought me a kind and very feeling letter from the poor Queen. I feel very much for her, and really feel that the poor good King was always so kind personally to me, that I should be ungrateful were I not to recollect it and feel grieved at his death. The poor Queen is wonderfully composed now, I hear.

Wrote my journal. Took my dinner upstairs alone. Went downstairs. Saw Stockmar. At about twenty minutes to 9 came Lord Melbourne and remained till near 10. I had a very important and a very *comfortable* conversation with him. Each time I see him I feel more confidence in him; I find him very kind in his manner too. Saw Stockmar. Went down and said good-night to Mamma, etc. My *dear* Lehzen will *always* remain with me as my friend, but will take no situation about me, and I think she is right.

From *The Letters of Queen Victoria*
edited by Benson and Esher

Nora

When Nora closed the door behind her in Ibsen's A Doll's House *(1879) its slam was said to be heard around the world. And still it reverberates. Henrik Ibsen succeeded in portraying the nineteenth century woman whose inner nature was in strong conflict with the role society imposed upon her.*

A Doll's House tells of Nora, wife and mother, treated by her husband (and by her father before that) as a charming toy, there to be cared for, of course, but primarily for their amusement. During a dangerous illness of her husband, Torvald Helmer, Nora, to save his life, secretly borrows money and forges the name of her dying father so as not to distress him. Helmer recovers after a year in Italy paid for, he thinks, with his father-in-law's money.

Nora, happy at having helped save her husband's life, continues to make secret payments on her loan by hidden economies, and when the play opens has almost paid it off. To her joy, her husband has just been named manager of his bank. Life would continue as before in the doll house.

Krogstad, Nora's creditor, and an employee at the bank, however, blackmails Nora into trying to persuade Helmer to give him a promotion. Nora, by now aware of the gravity of her forgery, in her romantic way hopes that a miracle will happen whereby Helmer will attempt to take upon himself the blame for her action when he learns of it—not that she intends to let him.

Helmer finds out after they return from a ball. Rather than being grateful to Nora and trying to protect her, he castigates her and her dead father. Rapidly he begins to make plans how to protect himself by hushing up the matter.

With cold calmness Nora sees her husband in a new light. In the middle of their heated exchange comes a note from Krogstad returning Nora's I.O.U. Then Helmer is willing to forgive her. But by then, Nora, hardly in need of forgiveness, knows this is not a man she loves. She is finished being a doll-wife. She leaves Helmer that very evening because of what she calls "my duties toward myself."

ELLEN. (*Half dressed, in the hall.*) Here is a letter for you, ma'am.

HELMER. Give it to me. (*Seizes the letter and shuts the door.*) Yes, from him. You shall not have it. I shall read it.

NORA. Read it!

HELMER. (*By the lamp.*) I have hardly the courage to. We may both be lost, both you and I. Ah! I must know. (*Hastily tears the letter open; reads a few lines, looks at an enclosure; with a cry of joy*) Nora! (*Nora looks inquiringly at him.*)

HELMER. Nora!—Oh! I must read it again.—Yes, yes, it is so. I am saved! Nora, I am saved!

NORA. And I?

HELMER. You too, of course; we are both saved, both of us. Look here—he sends you back your promissory note. He writes that he regrets and apologizes that a happy turn in his life— Oh, what matter what he writes. We are saved, Nora! No one can harm you. Oh, Nora, Nora— but first to get rid of this hateful thing. I'll just see— (*Glances at the I.O.U.*) No, I will not look at it; the whole thing shall be nothing but a dream to me (*Tears the I.O.U. and both letters in pieces. Throws them into the fire and watches them burn.*) There! It's gone!—He said that ever since Christmas Eve— Oh, Nora, they must have been three terrible days for you!

NORA. I have fought a hard fight for the last three days.

HELMER. And in your agony you saw no other outlet but— No; we won't think of that horror. We will only rejoice and repeat— it's over, all over! Don't you hear, Nora? You don't seem able to grasp it. Yes, it's over. What is this set look on your face? Oh, my poor Nora, I understand; you cannot believe that I have for-

given you. But I have, Nora; I swear it. I have forgiven everything. I know that what you did was all for love of me.

NORA. That is true.

HELMER. You loved me as a wife should love her husband. It
was only the means that, in your inexperience, you misjudged.
But do you think I love you the less because you cannot do
without guidance? No, no. Only lean on me. I will counsel you,
and guide you. I should be no true man if this very womanly
helplessness did not make you doubly dear in my eyes. You
mustn't dwell upon the hard things I said in my first moment of
terror, when the world seemed to be tumbling about my ears. I
have forgiven you, Nora—I swear I have forgiven you.

NORA. I thank you for your forgiveness. (*Goes out, to the right.*)

HELMER. No, stay— (*Looking through the doorway.*) What are
you going to do?

NORA. (*Inside.*) To take off my masquerade dress.

HELMER. (*In the doorway.*) Yes, do, dear. Try to calm down,
and recover your balance, my scared little song-bird. You may
rest secure. I have broad wings to shield you. (*Walking up and
down near the door.*) Oh, how lovely—how cosy our home is,
Nora! Here you are safe; here I can shelter you like a hunted
dove whom I have saved from the claws of the hawk. I shall soon
bring your poor beating heart to rest; believe me, Nora, very
soon. Tomorrow all this will seem quite different—everything
will be as before. I shall not need to tell you again that I forgive
you; you will feel for yourself that it is true. How could you
think it in my heart to drive you away, or even so much as to
reproach you? Oh, you don't know a true man's heart, Nora.
There is something indescribably sweet and soothing to a man
in having forgiven his wife—honestly forgiven her, from the
bottom of his heart. She becomes his property in a double sense.
She is as though born again; she has become, so to speak, at
once his wife and his child. That is what you shall henceforth be
to me, my bewildered, helpless darling. Don't be troubled about

anything, Nora; only open your heart to me, and I will be both
will and conscience to you. (*Nora enters in everyday dress.*) Why,
what's this? Not gone to bed? You have changed your dress?
NORA. Yes, Torvald; now I have changed my dress.
HELMER. But why now, so late?
NORA. I shall not sleep tonight.
HELMER. But, Nora dear—
NORA. (*Looking at her watch.*) It's not so late yet. Sit down,
Torvald; you and I have much to say to each other. (*She sits at
one side of the table.*)
HELMER. Nora—what does this mean? Your cold, set face—
NORA. Sit down. It will take some time. I have much to talk
over with you. (*Helmer sits at the other side of the table.*)
HELMER. You alarm me, Nora. I don't understand you.
NORA. No, that is just it. You don't understand me; and I have
never understood you—till to-night. No, don't interrupt. Only
listen to what I say. We must come to a final settlement, Torvald.
HELMER. How do you mean?
NORA. (*After a short silence.*) Does not one thing strike you as
we sit here?
HELMER. What should strike me?
NORA. We have been married eight years. Does it not strike you
that this is the first time we two, you and I, man and wife, have
talked together seriously?
HELMER. Seriously! What do you call seriously?
NORA. During eight whole years, and more—ever since the day
we first met—we have never exchanged one serious word about
serious things.
HELMER. Was I always to trouble you with the cares you could
not help me to bear?
NORA. I am not talking of cares. I say that we have never yet
set ourselves seriously to get to the bottom of anything.
HELMER. Why, my dearest Nora, what have you to do with
serious things?

NORA. There we have it! You have never understood me. I have had great injustice done me, Torvald; first by father, and then by you.

HELMER. What! By your father and me? By us, who have loved you more than all the world?

NORA. (*Shaking her head.*) You have never loved me. You only thought it amusing to be in love with me.

HELMER. Why, Nora, what a thing to say!

NORA. Yes, it is so, Torvald. While I was at home with father, he used to tell me all his opinions, and I held the same opinions. If I had others I said nothing about them, because he wouldn't have liked it. He used to call me his doll-child, and played with me as I played with my dolls. Then I came to live in your house—

HELMER. What an expression to use about our marriage!

NORA. (*Undisturbed.*) I mean I passed from father's hands into yours. You arranged everything according to your taste; and I got the same tastes as you; or I pretended to—I don't know which—both ways, perhaps; sometimes one and sometimes the other. When I look back on it now, I seem to have been living here like a beggar, from hand to mouth. I lived by performing tricks for you, Torvald. But you would have it so. You and father have done me a great wrong. It is your fault that my life has come to nothing.

HELMER. Why, Nora, how unreasonable and ungrateful you are! Have you not been happy here?

NORA. No, never. I thought I was; but I never was.

HELMER. Not—not happy!

NORA. No; only merry. But you have always been so kind to me. But our house has been nothing but a play room. Here I have been your doll-wife, just as at home I used to be papa's doll-child. And the children, in their turn, have been my dolls. I thought it fun when you played with me, just as the children did when I played with them. That has been our marriage, Torvald.

HELMER. There is some truth in what you say, exaggerated and overstrained though it be. But henceforth it shall be different. Play-time is over; now comes the time for education.

NORA. Whose education? Mine, or the children's?

HELMER. Both, my dear Nora.

NORA. Oh, Torvald, you are not the man to teach me to be a fit wife for you.

HELMER. And you can say that?

NORA. And I—how have I prepared myself to educate the children?

HELMER. Nora!

NORA. Did you not say yourself, a few minutes ago, you dared not trust them to me?

HELMER. In the excitement of the moment! Why should you dwell upon that?

NORA. No—you were perfectly right. That problem is beyond me. There is another to be solved first—I must try to educate myself. You are not the man to help me in that. I must set about it alone. And that is why I am leaving you.

HELMER. (Jumping up.) What—do you mean to say?

NORA. I must stand quite alone if I am ever to know myself and my surroundings; so I cannot stay with you.

HELMER. Nora! Nora!

NORA. I am going at once. I daresay Christina will take me in for to-night.

HELMER. You are mad! I shall not allow it! I forbid it!

NORA. It is of no use your forbidding me anything. I shall take with me what belongs to me. From you I will accept nothing, either now or afterwards.

HELMER. What madness this is!

NORA. Tomorrow I shall go home—I mean to what was my home. It will be easier for me to find some opening there.

HELMER. Oh, in your blind inexperience—

NORA. I must try to gain experience, Torvald.

HELMER. To forsake your home, your husband, and your children. And you don't consider what the world will say.

NORA. I can pay no heed to that. I only know that I must do it.

HELMER. This is monstrous! Can you forsake your holiest duties in this way?

NORA. What do you consider my holiest duties?

HELMER. Do I need to tell you that? Your duties to your husband and your children.

NORA. I have other duties equally sacred.

HELMER. Impossible! What duties do you mean?

NORA. My duties towards myself.

HELMER. Before all else you are a wife and a mother.

NORA. That I no longer believe. I believe that before all else I am a human being, just as much as you are—or at least that I should try to become one. I know that most people agree with you, Torvald, and that they say so in books. But henceforth I can't be satisfied with what most people say, and what is in books. I must think things out for myself, and try to get clear about them.

HELMER. Are you not clear about your place in your own home? Have you not an infallible guide in questions like these? Have you not religion?

NORA. Oh, Torvald, I don't really know what religion is.

HELMER. What do you mean?

NORA. I know nothing but what Pastor Hansen told me when I was confirmed. He explained that religion was this and that. When I get away from all this and stand alone, I will look into that matter too. I will see whether what he taught me is right or, at any rate, whether it is right for me.

HELMER. Oh, this is unheard of! And from so young a woman! But if religion cannot keep you right, let me appeal to your conscience—for I suppose you have some moral feeling? Or, answer me: perhaps you have none?

NORA. Well, Torvald, it's not easy to say. I really don't know—

I am all at sea about these things. I only know that I think quite differently from you about them. I hear, too, that the laws are different from what I thought; but I can't believe that they can be right. It appears that a woman has no right to spare her dying father, or to save her husband's life! I don't believe that.

HELMER. You talk like a child. You don't understand the society in which you live.

NORA. No, I do not. But now I shall try to learn. I must make up my mind which is right—society or I.

HELMER. Nora, you are ill; you are feverish; I almost think you are out of your senses.

NORA. I have never felt so much clearness and certainty as tonight.

HELMER. You are clear and certain enough to forsake husband and children?

NORA. Yes, I am.

HELMER. Then there is only one explanation possible.

NORA. What is it?

HELMER. You no longer love me.

NORA. No; that is just it.

HELMER. Nora!—Can you say so!

NORA. Oh, I'm so sorry, Torvald; for you've always been so kind to me. But I can't help it. I do not love you any longer.

HELMER. (*Mastering himself with difficulty.*) Are you clear and certain on this point too?

NORA. Yes, quite. That is why I will not stay here any longer.

HELMER. And can you also make clear to me how I have forfeited your love?

NORA. Yes, I can. It was this evening, when the miracle did not happen; for then I saw you were not the man I had imagined.

HELMER. Explain yourself more clearly; I don't understand.

NORA. I have waited so patiently all these eight years; for of course I saw clearly enough that miracles don't happen every day. When this crushing blow threatened me, I said to myself so confidently, "Now comes the miracle!" When Krogstad's letter lay in the box, it never for a moment occurred to me that you would think of submitting to that man's conditions. I was convinced that you would say to him, "Make it known to all the world"; and that then—

HELMER. Well? When I had given my own wife's name up to disgrace and shame?

NORA. Then I firmly believed that you would come forward, take everything upon yourself, and say, "I am the guilty one."

HELMER. Nora!

NORA. You mean I would never have accepted such a sacrifice? No, certainly not. But what would my assertions have been worth in opposition to yours?—that was the miracle that I hoped for and dreaded. And it was to hinder that that I wanted to die.

HELMER. I would gladly work for you day and night. Nora— bear sorrow and want for your sake. But no man sacrifices his honour, even for one he loves.

NORA. Millions of women have done so.

HELMER. Oh, you think and talk like a silly child.

NORA. Very likely. But you neither think nor talk like the man I can share my life with. When your terror was over—not for what threatened me, but for yourself—when there was nothing more to fear—then it seemed to you as though nothing had happened. I was your lark again, your doll, just as before—whom you would take twice as much care of in future, because she was so weak and fragile. (*Stands up.*) Torvald—in that moment it burst upon me that I had been living here these eight years with a strange man, and had borne him three children. Oh, I can't bear to think of it! I could tear myself to pieces!

HELMER. (*Sadly.*) I see it, I see it; an abyss has opened between us. But, Nora, can it never be filled up?

NORA. As I now am, I am no wife for you.

HELMER. I have strength to become another man.

NORA. Perhaps—when your doll is taken away from you.

HELMER. To part—to part from you! No, Nora, no; I can't grasp the thought.

NORA. (*Going into room on the right.*) The more reason for the thing to happen. (*She comes back with outdoor things and a small travelling bag, which she places on a chair.*)

HELMER. Nora, Nora, not now! Wait till to-morrow.

NORA. (*Putting on cloak*) I can't spend the night in a strange man's house.

HELMER. But can we not live here, as brother and sister?

NORA. (*Fastening her hat.*) You know very well that wouldn't last long. (*Puts on the shawl.*) Good-bye, Torvald. No, I won't go to the children. I know they are in better hands than mine. As I now am, I can be nothing to them.

HELMER. But sometime, Nora—sometime?

NORA. How can I tell? I have no idea what will become of me.

HELMER. But you are my wife, now and always!

NORA. Listen, Torvald—when a wife leaves her husband's house, as I am doing, I have heard that in the eyes of the law he is free from all duties towards her. At any rate, I release you from all duties. You must not feel yourself bound, any more than I shall. There must be perfect freedom on both sides. There, I give you back your ring. Give me mine.

HELMER. That too?

NORA. That too.

HELMER. Here it is.

NORA. Very well. Now it is all over. I lay the keys here. The servants know about everything in the house—better than I do. To-morrow, when I have started, Christina will come to pack up the things I brought with me from home. I will have them sent after me.

HELMER. All over! All over! Nora, will you never think of me again?

NORA. Oh, I shall often think of you, and the children, and this house.

HELMER. May I write to you, Nora?

NORA. No—never. You must not.

HELMER. But I must send you—

NORA. Nothing, nothing.

HELMER. I must help you if you need it.

NORA. No, I say. I take nothing from strangers.

HELMER. Nora—can I never be more than a stranger to you?

NORA. (*Taking her travelling-bag*) Oh, Torvald, then the miracle of miracles would have to happen—

HELMER. What is the miracle of miracles?

NORA. Both of us would have to change so that—Oh, Torvald, I no longer believe in miracles.

HELMER. But I will believe. Tell me! We must so change that—

NORA. That communion between us shall be a marriage. Good-bye. (*She goes out by the hall door.*)

HELMER. (*Sinks into a chair by the door with his face in his hands.*) Nora! Nora! (*He looks round and rises.*) Empty. She is gone. (*A hope springs up in him.*) Ah! The miracle of miracles—! (*From below is heard the reverberation of a heavy door closing.*)

From *A Doll's House* by Henrik Isben

Harriet Beecher Stowe

Daughter of a Congregational clergyman, Lyman Beecher, and sister of Henry Ward Beecher, Harriet Beecher Stowe (1811–1896) grew up in an atmosphere that fostered her interest in matters theological and humanitarian.

She married Calvin Ellis Stowe, a college professor (under-practical and over-generous), and although they were always to be plagued by financial worries theirs was a marriage of deep love. In a letter to her when she was away he wrote, "I am daily finding out more and more (what I knew very well before) that you are the most intelligent and agreeable woman in the whole circle of my acquaintance." And she to him: ". . . I did not know till I came away how much I was dependent upon you for information. There are a thousand favorite subjects on which I could talk with you better than anyone else. If you were not already my dearly loved husband I should certainly fall in love with you."

It was he who suggested to her that she write and her first work, which brought her world-wide fame and promoted the cause of anti-slavery, Uncle Tom's Cabin, *sold 300,000 copies in the first year.*

She and her husband had six children. Immediately after her return from one of her trips to England her oldest son, Henry Ellis, was drowned while swimming in the Connecticut River at Hanover, New Hampshire, where he was a freshman at Dartmouth. Mrs. Stowe shared her sorrow in a letter to her friend, the Duchess of Sutherland.

August 3, 1857

DEAR FRIEND—Before this reaches you you will have perhaps learned from other sources of the sad blow which has fallen upon us—our darling, our good, beautiful boy, snatched away in the moment of health and happiness. Alas! could I know that when I parted from my Henry on English shores that I should never see him more? I returned to my home, and, amid the jubilee of meeting the rest, was fain to be satisfied with only a letter from him, saying that his college examinations were coming on, and he must defer seeing me a week or two till they were over. I thought then of taking his younger brother and going up to visit him; but the health of the latter seeming unfavorably affected by the seacoast air, I turned back with him to a water-cure establishment. Before I had been two weeks absent a fatal telegram hurried me home, and when I arrived there it was to find the house filled with his weeping classmates, who had just come bringing his remains. There he lay so calm, so placid, so peaceful, that I could not believe that he would not smile upon me, and that my voice which always had such power over him could not recall him. There had always been such a peculiar union, such a tenderness between us. I had had such power always to call up answering feelings to my own, that it seemed impossible that he could be silent and unmoved at my grief. But yet, dear friend, I am sensible that in this last sad scene I had an alleviation that was not granted to you. I recollect, in the mournful letter you wrote me about that time, you said that you mourned that you had never told your own dear one how much you loved him. That sentence touched me at the time. I laid it to heart, and from that time lost no occasion of expressing to my children those feelings that we too often defer to express to our dearest friends till it is forever too late.

He did fully know how I loved him, and some of the last loving words he spoke were of me. The very day that he was taken from us, and when he was just rising from the table of his boarding-house to go whence he never returned, some one noticed the seal ring, which you may remember to have seen on his finger, and said, How beautiful that ring is! Yes, he said, and best of all,

it was my mother's gift to me. That ring, taken from the life-
less hand a few hours later, was sent to me. Singularly enough,
it is broken right across the name from a fall a little time
previous. . . .

It is a great comfort to me, dear friend, that I took Henry with
me to Dunrobin. I hesitated about keeping him so long from his
studies, but still I thought a mind so observing and appreciative
might learn from such a tour more than through books, and so
it was. He returned from England full of high resolves and manly
purposes. "I may not be what the world calls a Christian," he
wrote, "but I will live such a life as a Christian ought to live,
such a life as every true man ought to live." Henceforth he became remarkable for a strict order and energy, and a vigilant
temperance and care of his bodily health, docility and deference
to his parents and teachers, and perseverance in every duty. . . .
Well, from the hard battle of this life he is excused, and the will
is taken for the deed, and whatever comes his heart will not be
pierced as mine is. But I am glad that I can connect him with all
my choicest remembrances of the Old World. . . .

From *The Life of Harriet Beecher Stowe*
by Charles Edward Stowe

Rosa Luxemburg

A woman of brain, heart, will, passion, Rosa Luxemburg (1871–1919) was a revolutionary born in Russian Poland but by marriage a German citizen. Daughter of a Jewish intelléctual family she identified actively even in her teens with the workers' problems. Under threat of imprisonment and possible banishment to Siberia she was smuggled over the Russian-German border to Switzerland before she was nineteen. The stratagem used was to enlist the help of a local Catholic priest who was led to believe that she was a Jewish girl ardently wishing to become a Christian but unable because of parental opposition. The priest helped to smuggle her out under the straw of a peasant's cart.

A brilliant writer and orator, she participated in the revolution in Russian Poland in 1905, and was active in the Second International. In 1906 she underwent her first imprisonment. With Karl Liebknecht she helped to form the Spartacus Party in Germany during World War I, and in 1918 aided in its transformation into the German Communist party. For her part in the Spartacus uprising in Berlin she was arrested in January, 1919. As Rosa Luxemburg was taken from the hotel where the arrest had been made, an officer under orders smashed her skull with his rifle-butt and threw her into a car where she was shot to death. Her corpse was then thrown into a canal where it washed up four months later.

In 1915 she spent some time in the women's prison in the Berlin Barnimstrasse. In a letter to her friend and secretary, Mathilde Jacob, she describes her first day there.

✳ EVEN the journey in the Black Maria didn't shake me up; after all, I had experienced exactly the same ride in Warsaw. Indeed, it was such a strikingly similar situation that it started a train of various cheerful thoughts. To be sure, there was one difference this time: the Russian gendarmes had escorted me with great respect as a "political," whereas the Berlin police declared they didn't give a damn ("schnuppe") who I was, and stuck me into the car with my new "colleagues." Ah well, these are all piddling matters in the end; and never forget that life should be taken with serenity and cheerfulness. Incidentally, so that you don't get any exaggerated ideas about my heroism, I'll confess, repentently, that when I had to strip to my chemise and submit to a frisking for the second time that day, I could barely hold back the tears. Of course, deep inside, I was furious with myself at such weakness, and I still am. Also on that first evening, what really dismayed me was not the prison cell and my sudden exclusion from the land of the living, but—take a guess!—the fact that I had to go to bed without a night-dress and without having combed my hair. And, so as not to omit a quotation from the classics: do you remember the first scene in "Mary Stuart," when Mary's trinkets are taken away from her? "To do without life's little ornaments," says her nurse, Lady Kennedy, "is harder than to brave great trials." (Do look it up; Schiller put it rather more beautifully than I have here.) But where are my errant thoughts leading me? *Gott strafe England* and may He forgive me for comparing myself with an English queen.

From *Rosa Luxemburg—Ideas in Action*
by Paul Frolich

Sylvia Plath

Almost all Sylvia Plath's (1932–1963) published pictures show her apparently as a happy person, certainly as an attractive person. In a journal excerpt written at seventeen she declares, "I am very happy." Yet before completing her degree at Smith she had a severe breakdown, followed by shock treatment, and before she was thirty-two, worn out by illness, overwork, anxiety, she was to take her life in London.

When she was happy, was it possible that she was too intensely happy? If so, did this, then, make the less happy times seem too grim?

She had much to make her happy. Graduation *summa cum laude from Smith and a Fulbright scholarship to Cambridge. Publication and literary awards. Marriage to English poet Ted Walker. With the literary successes, however, came also the rejection slips. And after six years of marriage, she and her husband separated, their two children remaining in her care.*

Her first volume of poetry, The Collosus, *well-crafted and intensely personal, was published in 1960.* Ariel, *which is considered her finest book of poetry, was written in the last months of her life, and published posthumously, as were* Crossing the Water *and* Winter Trees.

Her one novel, The Bell Jar *(1963) was originally published in England under the pseudonym, Victoria Lucas. It is autobiographical in that it is a fictionalized account of the nervous breakdown she suffered in college.*

For a number of years, as Sylvia was growing up, it was her mother's custom to slip a diary into her Christmas stocking. At thirteen she asked her mother henceforth to give her an undated journal rather than a dated diary because, "When the big moments come, one page is not enough."

✳ As of today I have decided to keep a diary again—just a place where I can write my thoughts and opinions when I have a moment. Somehow I have to keep and hold the rapture of being seventeen. Every day is so precious I feel infinitely sad at the thought of all this time melting farther and farther away from me as I grow older. *Now, now* is the perfect time of my life.

In reflecting back upon these last sixteen years, I can see tragedies and happiness, all relative—all unimportant now—fit only to smile upon a bit mistily.

I still do not know myself. Perhaps I never will. But I feel free—unbound by responsibility. I still can come up to my own private room, with my drawings hanging on the walls . . . and pictures pinned up over my bureau. It is a room suited to me—tailored, uncluttered and peaceful. . . . I love the quiet lines of the furniture, the two bookcases filled with poetry books and fairy tales saved from childhood.

At the present moment I am very happy, sitting at my desk, looking out at the bare trees around the house across the street. . . . Always I want to be an observer. I want to be affected by life deeply, but never so blinded that I cannot see my share of existence in a wry, humorous light and mock myself as I mock others.

I am afraid of getting older. I am afraid of getting married. Spare me from cooking three meals a day—spare me from the relentless cage of routine and rote. I want to be free—free to know people and their backgrounds—free to move to different parts of the world so I may learn that there are other morals and standards besides my own. I want, I think, to be omniscient . . . I think I would like to call myself "The girl who wanted to be God." Yet if I were not in this body, where *would* I be—perhaps I am *destined* to be classified and qualified. But, oh, I cry out against it. I am I—I am powerful—but to what extent? I am I.

Sometimes I try to put myself in another's place, and I am

frightened when I find I am almost succeeding. How awful to be anyone but I. I have a terrible egotism. I love my flesh, my face, my limbs with overwhelming devotion. I know that I am "too tall" and have a fat nose, and yet I pose and prink before the mirror seeing more and more how lovely I am . . . I have erected in my mind an image of myself—idealistic and beautiful. Is not that image, free from blemish, the true self—the true perfection? Am I wrong when this image insinuates itself between me and the merciless mirror? (Oh, even now I glance back on what I have just written—how foolish it sounds, how overdramatic.)

Never, never, never will I reach the perfection I long for with all my soul—my paintings, my poems, my stories—all poor, poor reflections . . . for I have been too thoroughly conditioned to the conventional surroundings of this community . . . my vanity desires luxuries which I can never have. . . .

I am continually more aware of the power which chance plays in my life. . . . There will come a time when I must face myself at last. Even now I dread the big choices which loom up in my life—what college? What career? I am afraid. I feel uncertain. What is best for me? What do I want? I do not know. I love freedom. I deplore constrictions and limitations. . . . I am not as wise as I have thought. I can now see, as from a valley, the roads lying open for me, but I cannot see the end—the consequences. . . .

Oh, I love *now*, with all my fears and forebodings, for *now* I still am not completely molded. My life is still just beginning. I am strong. I long for a cause to devote my energies to. . . .

From *Letters Home* by Sylvia Plath,
edited by Aurelia Schober Plath

Mary McLeod Bethune

Mary McLeod Bethune (1875–1955), born in Mayesville, South Carolina, was the fifteenth child of former slaves, and the first of them to be born free. From the beginning her parents regarded her as a child destined to do something special.

Less than ten years after graduation from the Moody Bible Institute in Chicago she founded, in Florida, the Daytona Normal and Industrial Institute for Negro Girls, which in 1923 merged with Cookman Institute to become Bethune-Cookman College.

American presidents—Coolidge, Hoover, Roosevelt—turned to her for advice on the education of blacks. Under Franklin Roosevelt she was Director of Negro Affairs of the National Youth Administration and served as the President's special advisor on minority affairs.

❋ To Mrs. Bethune's mind there was a marked distinction between being the first *woman* to occupy her many distinguished positions and being the only *Negro* to receive the many honors that were bestowed upon her. As a trail blazer, she took pride in the former, but deplored the state of society which made the latter remarkable.

A note from her diary reads: "December 9, 1937 Tuesday at five in the afternoon I attended a tea at the Executive Mansion." This was an annual occasion at which Mrs. Roosevelt entertained the women administrative workers in the government.

One curious but affable woman inquired of her, "Who are you?"

"My name is Mary McLeod Bethune."

"What do you do?"

"I am the director of Negro Affairs in the NYA."

"Isn't it nice of Mrs. Roosevelt to have you here."

"Yes, isn't it nice of Mrs. Roosevelt to have *all* of us here!"

The diary continues: "While I felt very much at home, I looked about me longingly for other dark faces. In all that great group I felt a sense of being quite alone.

"Then I thought how vitally important it was that I be here, to help these others get used to seeing us in high places. And so, while I sip tea in the brilliance of the White House, my heart reaches out to the delta land and the bottom land.

"I know so well why I *must* be here, *must* go to tea at the White House. To remind them always that we belong here, we are a part of this America."

From *Mary McLeod Bethune* by Rackham Holt

Lillian Hellman

Lillian Hellman (1905–   ) is one of America's greatest playwrights; her works include The Children's Hour, The Little Foxes, Another Part of the Forest *and* Watch on the Rhine. *In 1952, the year when Senator Joseph McCarthy appeared at the top of his power, she was summoned to testify on her putatively un-American activities before the House Un-American Activities Committee (HUAC).*

The Committee was bent upon flushing out whatever it regarded as dangerous, un-American activity. It did not scruple about its means. Nor did it concern itself with the ruined lives of those wrongly investigated. Often, in its hearings room there took place a type of Children's Hour, *played by adults. The Committee fitted comfortably into the McCarthy Era, and the period quickly became one in which a number of people, in order to save job or prestige, named the guiltless before the Committee in order to illumine their own guiltlessness.*

Not so Lillian Hellman! And in a letter she sent to the Committee after her summons, she wrote, "I cannot and will not cut my conscience to fit this year's fashions." Further, she notified the Committee before her appearance that she would take the Fifth Amendment only if forced to name others.

She had drawn the Red-hunters' eye by her sponsorship of the Cultural and Scientific Conference for World Peace held at the Waldorf-Astoria Hotel in the spring of 1940. Other things could have led them to her earlier. She was prominent in the Henry Wallace campaign for the presidency. She had lived for decades with Dashiell Hammett, who may have been a Communist, and who, a year before her summons, had refused to name contributors to a Civil Rights Congress bail fund, and was sent to jail for contempt.

In writing of Ms. Hellman's experience with the Committee, Garry Wills says: "Despite her literary stature, she seems an unlikely heroine for that grim time, a blend of sassy kid and Southern lady, scared but defiant in her Balmain 'testifying dress.' But we must remember that Dashiell Hammett modeled Nora Charles after her in The Thin Man.*" Nora, elegant and sophisticated, could be when necessary "one tough lady."*

❋ THE Committee room was almost empty except for a few elderly, small-faced ladies sitting in the rear. They looked as if they were permanent residents and, since they occasionally spoke to each other, it was not too long a guess that they came as an organized group or club. Clerks came in and out, put papers on the rostrum, and disappeared. I said maybe we had come too early, but Joe said no, it was better that I get used to the room.

Then, I think to make the wait better for me, he said, "Well, I can tell you now that in the early days of seeing you, I was scared that what happened to my friend might happen to me."

He stopped to tell Pollitt that he didn't understand about the press—not one newspaperman had appeared.

I said, "What happened to your friend?"

"He represented a Hollywood writer who told him that he would under no circumstances be a friendly witness. That was why my friend took the case. So they get here, in the same seats we are, sure of his client, and within ten minutes the writer is one of the friendliest witnesses the Committee has had the pleasure of. He throws in every name he can think of, including his college roommate, childhood friend."

I said, "No, that won't happen and for more solid reasons than your honor or mine. I told you I can't make quick changes."

Joe told Pollitt that he thought he understood about no press and the half-empty room: the Committee had kept our appearance as quiet as they could. Joe said, "That means they're frightened of us. I don't know whether that's good or bad, but we want the press here and I don't know how to get them."

He didn't have to know. The room suddenly began to fill up behind me and the press people began to push toward their section and were still piling in when Representative Wood began to pound his gavel. I hadn't seen the Committee come in, don't think I had realized that they were to sit on a raised platform, the government having learned from the stage, or maybe the other way around. I was glad I hadn't seen them come in—they made a gloomy picture. Through the noise of the gavel I heard one of the ladies in the rear cough very loudly. She was to cough all through the hearing. Later I heard one of her friends say loudly, "Irma, take your good cough drops."

The opening questions were standard: what was my name, where was I born, what was my occupation, what were the titles of my plays. It didn't take long to get to what really interested them: my time in Hollywood, which studios I had worked for, what periods of what years, with some mysterious emphasis on 1937. (My time in Spain, I thought, but I was wrong.)

Had I met a writer called Martin Berkeley? (I had never, still have never, met Martin Berkeley, although Hammett told me later that I had once sat at a lunch table of sixteen or seventeen people with him in the old Metro-Goldwyn-Mayer commissary.) I said I must refuse to answer that question. Mr. Tavenner said he'd like to ask me again whether I had stated I was abroad in the summer of 1937. I said yes, explained that I had been in New York for several weeks before going to Europe, and got myself ready for what I knew was coming: Martin Berkeley, one of the Committee's most lavish witnesses on the subject of Hollywood, was now going to be put to work. Mr. Tavenner read Berkeley's testimony. Perhaps he is worth quoting, the small details are nicely formed, even about his "old friend Hammett," who had no more than a bowing acquaintance with him.

MR. TAVENNER: . . . I would like you to tell the committee when and where the Hollywood section of the Communist Party was first organized.

MR. BERKELEY: Well, sir, by a very strange coincidence the section was organized in my house. . . . In June of 1937, the middle of June, the meeting was held in my house. My house was picked because I had a large living room and ample parking facilities. . . . And it was a pretty good meeting. We were honored by the presence of many functionaries from downtown, and the spirit was swell. . . . Well, in addition to Jerome and the others I have mentioned before, and there is no sense in me going over the list again and again. . . . Also present was Harry Carlisle, who is now in the process of being deported, for which I am very grateful. He was an English subject. After Stanley Lawrence had stolen what funds there were from the party out here, and to make amends had gone to Spain and gotten himself killed, they sent Harry Carlisle here to conduct Marxist classes. . . . Also at the meeting was Donald Ogden Stewart. His name is spelled Donald Ogden S-t-e-w-a-r-t. Dorothy Parker, also a writer. Her husband Allen Campbell, C-a-m-p-b-e-l-l; my old friend Dashiell Hammett, who is now in jail in New York for his activities; that very excellent playwright Lillian Hellman . . .

And so on.

When this nonsense was finished, Mr. Tavenner asked me if it was true, I said that I wanted to refer to the letter I had sent, I would like the Committee to reconsider my offer in the letter.

MR. TAVENNER: In other words, you are asking the committee not to ask you any questions regarding the participation of other persons in the Communist Party activities?

I said I hadn't said that.

Mr. Wood said that in order to clarify the record Mr. Tavenner should put into the record the correspondence between me and the Committee. Mr. Tavenner did just that, and when he had finished Rauh sprang to his feet, picked up a stack of mimeographed copies of my letter, and handed them out to the press section. I was puzzled by this—I hadn't noticed he had the copies—but I did notice that Rauh was looking happy.

Mr. Tavenner was upset, far more than the printed words of my hearing show. Rauh said that Tavenner himself had put the letters in the record, and thus he thought passing out copies was proper. The polite words of each as they read on the page were not polite as spoken. I am convinced that in this section of the testimony, as in several other sections—certainly in Hammett's later testimony before the Senate Internal Security Subcommittee—either the court stenographer missed some of what was said and filled it in later, or the documents were, in part, edited. Having read many examples of the work of court stenographers, I have never once seen a completely accurate report.

Mr. Wood told Mr. Tavenner that the Committee could not be "placed in the attitude of trading with the witnesses as to what they will testify to" and that thus he thought both letters should be read aloud.

Mr. Tavenner did just this, and there was talk I couldn't hear, a kind of rustle, from the press section. Then Mr. Tavenner asked me if I had attended the meeting described by Berkeley, and one of the hardest things I ever did in my life was to swallow the words, "I don't know him and a little investigation into the time and place would have proved to you that I could not have been at the meeting he talks about." Instead, I said that I must refuse to answer the question. The "must" in that sentence annoyed Mr. Wood—it was to annoy him again and again—and he corrected me: "You might refuse to answer, the question is asked, do you refuse?"

But Wood's correction of me, the irritation in his voice, was making me nervous, and I began to move my right hand as if I had a tic, unexpected, and couldn't stop it. I told myself that if a word irritated him the insults would begin to come very soon. So I sat up straight, made my left hand hold my right hand, and hoped it would work. But I felt the sweat on my face and arms and knew that something was going to happen to me, something out of control, and I turned to Joe, remembering the suggested toilet intermission. But the clock said we had only been there sixteen minutes, and if it was going to come, the bad time, I had better hang on for a while.

Was I a member of the Communist party, had I been, what year had I stopped being? How could I harm such people as Martin Berkeley by admitting I had known them, and so on. At times I couldn't follow the reasoning, at times I understood full well that in refusing to answer questions about membership in the party I had, of course, trapped myself into a seeming admission that I once had been.

But in the middle of one of the questions about my past, something so remarkable happened that I am to this day convinced that the unknown gentleman who spoke had a great deal to do with the rest of my life. A voice from the press gallery had been for at least three or four minutes louder than the other voices. (By this time, I think, the press had finished reading my letter to the Committee and were discussing it.) The loud voice had been answered by a less loud voice, but no words could be distinguished. Suddenly a clear voice said, "Thank God somebody finally had the guts to do it."

It is never wise to say that something is the best minute of your life (you must be forgetting) but I still think that unknown voice made the words that helped to save me. (I had been sure that not only did the elderly ladies in the room disapprove of me, but the press would be antagonistic.) Wood rapped his gavel and said angrily, "If that occurs again, I will clear the press from these chambers."

"You do that, sir," said the same voice.

Mr. Wood spoke to somebody over his shoulder and the somebody moved around to the press section, but that is all that happened. To this day I don't know the name of the man who spoke, but for months later, almost every day I would say to myself, I wish I could tell him that I had really wanted to say to Mr. Wood: "There is no Communist menace in this country and you know it. You have made cowards into liars, an ugly business, and you made me write a letter in which I acknowledged your power. I should have gone into your Committee room, given my name and address, and walked out." Many people have said they liked what I did, but I don't much, and if I hadn't worried about rats in jail, and such. . . . Ah, the bravery you tell yourself was possible when it's all over, the bravery of the staircase.

In the Committee room I heard Mr. Wood say, "Mr. Walter does not desire to ask the witness any further questions. Is there any reason why this witness should not be excused from further attendance before the Committee?"

Mr. Tavenner said, "No, sir."

My hearing was over an hour and seven minutes after it began. I don't think I understood that it was over, but Joe was whispering so loudly and so happily that I jumped from the noise in my ear.

. . . .

I called Hammett and left a message I'd be home for dinner. I didn't want to talk to him. I didn't want to say, even by inference, "See, I was right and you were wrong," because, of course, I had not been right, if by right one means what one wanted to say, didn't say, and the fact that I got off without being prosecuted didn't prove that I had been right.

I took a late afternoon plane to New York. I felt fine until I began to vomit after the takeoff. As I washed my face, I remembered Sophronia, my nurse, saying to the cook or to anybody else who could be trapped into listening about me, "The child's got no stomach. No matter how sick she is with what, she can't throw up. She try, I try, but it ain't to be."

From *Scoundrel Time* by Lillian Hellman

Emma Goldman

Emma Goldman (1869–1940) was a practicing anarchist, a labor agitator, a pacifist in World War I, an advocate of political violence, a feminist, a proponent of free love and birth control, and a Communist. I first learned of her from my American Government professor, a Dominican sister who had done her undergraduate work at the University of Wisconsin and who took inordinate glee in the fact that she had been suspended from the University for attending Emma Goldman's lecture after the students had been forbidden to go.

Goldman came to America from Russia when she was seventeen. After experiencing a sweat shop and an unfortunate marriage, she plunged herself into radical activity. From 1906 she edited, with Alexander Berkman, the anarchist paper, Mother Earth. *In 1916 she was imprisoned for publicly advocating birth control, and in 1917 for obstructing the draft.*

After World War I she was deported to Russia but in a few years left that country because of disagreement with the Bolshevik government. She was never permitted to live again in the United States but was allowed to lecture provided she did not publicly discuss politics.

She wrote her memoirs while living in Saint-Tropez, a picturesque fishing town on the French Riviera. Friends provided a fund to care for her material needs, a fund begun for her, interestingly enough, by Peggy Guggenheim.

❋ PRESENTLY Berkman remarked to me: "Johann Most is speaking tonight. Do you want to come to hear him?"

How extraordinary, I thought, that my very first day in New York I should have the chance to behold with my own eyes and hear the fiery man whom the Rochester press used to portray as the personification of the devil, a criminal, a blood-thirsty demon! I had planned to visit Most in the office of his newspaper some time later, but that the opportunity should present itself in such an unexpected manner gave me the feeling that something wonderful was about to happen, something that would decide the whole course of my life.

On the way to the hall I was too absorbed in my thoughts to hear much of the conversation that was going on between Berkman and the Minkin sisters. Suddenly I stumbled. I should have fallen had not Berkman gripped my arm and held me up. "I have saved your life," he said jestingly. "I hope I may be able to save yours some day," I quickly replied.

The meeting-place was a small hall behind a saloon, through which one had to pass. It was crowded with Germans, drinking, smoking, and talking. Before long, Johann Most entered. My first impression of him was one of revulsion. He was of medium height, with a large head crowned with greyish bushy hair; but his face was twisted out of form by an apparent dislocation of the left jaw. Only his eyes were soothing; they were blue and sympathetic.

His speech was a scorching denunciation of American conditions, a biting satire on the injustice and brutality of the dominant powers, a passionate tirade against those responsible for the Haymarket tragedy and the execution of the Chicago anarchists in November 1887. He spoke eloquently and picturesquely. As if by magic, his disfigurement disappeared, his lack of physical distinction was forgotten. He seemed transformed into some primitive power, radiating hatred and love, strength and inspiration. The rapid current of his speech, the music of his voice, and his sparkling wit, all combined to produce an effect almost overwhelming. He stirred me to my depths.

Caught in the crowd that surged towards the platform, I found myself before Most. Berkman was near me and introduced me. But I was dumb with excitement and nervousness, full of the tumult of emotions Most's speech had aroused in me.

That night I could not sleep. Again I lived through the events of 1887. Twenty-one months had passed since the Black Friday of November 11, when the Chicago men had suffered their martyrdom, yet every detail stood out clear before my vision and affected me as if it had happened but yesterday. My sister Helena and I had become interested in the fate of the men during the period of their trial. The reports in the Rochester newspapers irritated, confused, and upset us by their evident prejudice. The violence of the press, the bitter denunciation of the accused, the attacks on all foreigners, turned our sympathies to the Haymarket victims.

We had learned of the existence in Rochester of a German socialist group that held sessions on Sunday in Germania Hall. We began to attend the meetings, my older sister, Helena, on a few occasions only, and I regularly. The gatherings were generally uninteresting, but they offered an escape from the grey dullness of my Rochester existence. There one heard, at least, something different from the everlasting talk about money and business, and one met people of spirit and ideas.

One Sunday it was announced that a famous socialist speaker from New York, Johanna Greie, would lecture on the case then being tried in Chicago. On the appointed day I was the first in the hall. The huge place was crowded from top to bottom by eager men and women, while the walls were lined with police. I had never before been at such a large meeting. I had seen *gendarmes* in St. Petersburg disperse small student gatherings. But that in the country which guaranteed free speech, officers armed with long clubs should invade an orderly assembly filled me with consternation and protest.

Soon the chairman announced the speaker. She was a woman in her thirties, pale and ascetic-looking, with large luminous eyes. She spoke with great earnestness, in a voice vibrating with intensity. Her manner engrossed me. I forgot the police, the audience, and everything else about me. I was aware only of the frail woman in black crying out her passionate indictment against the forces that were about to destroy eight human lives.

The entire speech concerned the stirring events in Chicago. She began by relating the historical background of the case. She told of the labour strikes that broke out throughout the country in 1886, for the demand of an eight-hour workday. The centre of the movement was Chicago, and there the struggle between the toilers and their bosses became intense and bitter. A meeting of the striking employees of the McCormick Harvester Company in that city was attacked by police; men and women were beaten and several persons killed. To protest against the outrage a mass meeting was called in Haymarket Square on May 4. It was addressed by Albert Parsons, August Spies, Adolph Fischer, and others, and was quiet and orderly. This was attested to by Carter Harrison, Mayor of Chicago, who had attended the meeting to see what was going on. The Mayor left, satisfied that everything was all right, and he informed the captain of the district to that effect. It was getting cloudy, a light rain began to fall, and the people started to disperse, only a few remaining while one of the last speakers was addressing the audience. Then Captain Ward, accompanied by a strong force of police, suddenly appeared on the square. He ordered the meeting to disperse forthwith. "This is an orderly assembly," the chairman replied, whereupon the police fell upon the people, clubbing them unmercifully. Then something flashed through the air and exploded, killing a number of police officers and wounding a score of others. It was never ascertained who the actual culprit was, and the authorities apparently made little effort to discover him. Instead orders were immediately issued for the arrest of all the speakers at the Haymarket meeting and other prominent anarchists. The entire press and *bourgeoisie* of Chicago and of the whole country began shouting for the blood of the prisoners. A veritable campaign of terror was carried on by the police, who were given moral and financial encouragement by the Citizens' Association to further their murderous plan to get the anarchists out of the way. The public mind was so inflamed by the atrocious stories circulated by the press against the leaders of the strike that a fair trial for them became an impossibility. In fact, the trial proved the worst frame-up in the history of the United States. The jury was picked for conviction; the District Attorney announced in open court that it was not only the arrested men who were the accused, but that "anarchy was on trial" and that it was to be exterminated. The judge repeatedly denounced the prisoners from the bench, influencing the jury against them. The witnesses were terrorized or bribed, with the result that eight men, innocent of the crime and in no way connected with it, were convicted. The incited state of the public mind, and the general prejudice against anarchists, coupled with the employers' bitter opposition to the eight-hour movement, constituted the atmosphere that favoured the judicial murder of the Chicago anarchists. Five of them—Albert Parsons, August Spies, Louis Lingg, Adolph Fischer, and George Engel—were sentenced to die by hanging; Michael Schwab and Samuel Fielden were doomed to life imprisonment; Neebe received fifteen years' sentence. The innocent blood of the Haymarket martyrs was calling for revenge.

At the end of Greie's speech I knew what I had surmised all along: the Chicago men were innocent. They were to be put to death for their ideal. But what was their ideal? Johanna Greie spoke of Parsons, Spies, Lingg, and the others as socialists, but I was ignorant of the real meaning of socialism. What I had heard from the local speakers had impressed me as colourless and mechanistic. On the other hand, the papers called these men anarchist, bomb-throwers. What was anarchism? It was all very puzzling. But I had no time for further contemplation. The people were filing out, and I got up to leave. Greie, the chairman, and a group of friends were still on the platform. As I turned towards them, I saw Greie motioning to me. I was startled, my heart beat violently, and my feet felt leaden. When I approached her, she took me by the hand and said: "I never saw a face that reflected such a tumult of emotions as yours. You must be feeling the impending tragedy intensely. Do you know the men?" In a trembling voice I replied: "Unfortunately not, but I do feel the case with every fibre, and when I heard you speak, it seemed to me as if I knew them." She put her hand on my shoulder. "I have a feeling that you will know them better as you learn their ideal, and that you will make their cause your own."

I walked home in a dream. Sister Helena was already asleep, but I had to share my experience with her. I woke her up and recited to her the whole story, giving almost a verbatim account of the speech. I must have been very dramatic, because Helena exclaimed: "The next thing I'll hear about my little sister is that she, too, is a dangerous anarchist."

From *Living My Life* by Emma Goldman

Tess of the d'Urbervilles

Tess of the d'Urbervilles, *set in late nineteenth century England, was published in 1891. In this novel, Thomas Hardy probed the place of fate and its influence upon people's lives. If Tess's father had not learned he was a d'Urberville, if Angel had found the letter Tess had slipped under his door, would her life have been different?*

Jack Durbeyfield, laggard and ne'er-do-well, learns he is really descended from the famous d'Urberville family. Ceasing work completely he sends his daughter, Tess, to visit the Stoke-d'Urbervilles, a wealthy family which has assumed the name because no one else wants it. The son, Alec, forces his attentions upon Tess, and she becomes pregnant by him.

Tess returns to her home and although Alec pursues her she manages, by going to different farms to elude him and to give birth to her baby. At a dairy farm in the south she finds true love with Angel Clare, a pastor's son who has opted to study farming rather than the ministry. On the eve of their wedding night Tess slips under Angel's door a letter telling him about Alec and her. Angel does not find the letter, but Tess thinks that he has and that it has not changed their love.

On their wedding night Angel tells Tess about a debauched evening in his past. Tess forgives him, and then explains further about Alec and her. Angel is so shocked he says he cannot live with her. Taking her to her parents' home, he leaves for Brazil.

After the baby is born, Tess, with dignity and courage takes her place among the harvesters in the fields (the time in her life with which the following excerpt deals). She nurses her child there. Her love for him crests when she is about to lose him. Knowing she cannot save his life from the illness consuming him she is concerned what will happen to him if left unbaptized. Upon her father's refusal to summon the vicar, Tess christens the baby and calls him "Sorrow." Her child's name reflects the course of much of her life and its end.

✳ THE women—or rather girls, for they were mostly young— wore drawn cotton bonnets with great flapping curtains to keep off the sun, and gloves to prevent their hands being wounded by the stubble. There was one wearing a pale pink jacket, another in a cream-coloured tight-sleeved gown, another in a petticoat as red as the arms of the reaping-machine; and others, older, in the brown-rough "wrapper" or over-all—the old-established and most appropriate dress of the field-woman, which the young ones were abandoning. This morning the eye returns involuntarily to the girl in the pink cotton jacket, she being the most flexuous and finely drawn figure of them all. But her bonnet is pulled so far over her brow that none of her face is disclosed while she binds, though her complexion may be guessed from a stray twine or two of dark brown hair which extends below the curtain of her bonnet. Perhaps one reason why she seduces casual attention is that she never courts it, though the other women often gaze around them.

Her binding proceeds with clock-like monotony. From the sheaf last finished she draws a handful of ears, patting their tips with her left palm to bring them even. Then, stooping low, she moves forward, gathering the corn with both hands against her knees, and pushing her left gloved hand under the bundle to meet the right on the other side, holding the corn in an embrace like that of a lover. She brings the ends of the bond together, and kneels on the sheaf while she ties it, beating back her skirts now and then when lifted by the breeze. A bit of her naked arm is visible between the buff leather of the gauntlet and the sleeve of her gown; and as the day wears on its feminine smoothness becomes scarified by the stubble, and bleeds.

At intervals she stands up to rest, and to retie her disarranged apron, or to pull her bonnet straight. Then one can see the oval face of a handsome young woman with deep dark eyes and long, heavy, clinging tresses, which seem to clasp in a beseeching way anything they fall against. The cheeks are paler, the teeth more regular, the red lips thinner than is usual in a country-bred girl.

It is Tess Durbeyfield, otherwise d'Urberville, somewhat changed—the same, but not the same; at the present stage of her existence living as a stranger and an alien here, though it was no strange land that she was in. After a long seclusion she had come to a resolve to undertake outdoor work in her native village, the busiest season of the year in the agricultural world having arrived, and nothing that she could do within the house being so remunerative for the time as harvesting in the fields.

The movements of the other women were more or less similar to Tess's, the whole bevy of them drawing together like dancers in a quadrille at the completion of a sheaf by each, every one placing her sheaf on end against those of the rest, till a shock, or "stitch" as it was here called, of ten or a dozen was formed.

They went to breakfast, and came again, and the work proceeded as before. As the hour of eleven drew near a person watching her might have noticed that every now and then Tess's glance flitted wistfully to the brow of the hill, though she did not pause in her sheafing. On the verge of the hour the heads of a group of children, of ages ranging from six to fourteen, rose above the stubbly convexity of the hill.

The face of Tess flushed slightly, but still she did not pause.

The eldest of the comers, a girl who wore a triangular shawl, its corner dragging on the stubble, carried in her arms what at first sight seemed to be a doll, but proved to be an infant in long clothes. Another brought some lunch. The harvesters ceased working, took their provisions, and sat down against one of the shocks. Here they fell to, the men plying a stone jar freely, and passing round a cup.

Tess Durbeyfield had been one of the last to suspend her labours. She sat down at the end of the shock, her face turned somewhat away from her companions. When she had deposited herself a man in a rabbit-skin cap and with a handkerchief tucked into his belt, held the cup of ale over the top of the shock for her to drink. But she did not accept his offer. As soon as her lunch was spread she called up the big girl, her sister, and took the baby of her, who, glad to be relieved of the burden, went away to the next shock and joined the other children playing there. Tess, with a curiously stealthy yet courageous movement, and with a still rising colour, unfastened her frock and began suckling the child.

The men who sat nearest considerately turned their faces towards the other end of the field, some of them beginning to smoke; one, with absent-minded fondness, regretfully stroking the jar that would no longer yield a stream. All the women but Tess fell into animated talk, and adjusted the disarranged knots of their hair.

When the infant had taken its fill the young mother sat it upright in her lap, and looking into the far distance dandled it with a gloomy indifference that was almost dislike; then all of a sudden she fell to violently kissing it some dozens of times, as if she could never leave off, the child crying at the vehemence of an onset which strangely combined passionateness with contempt.

"She's fond of that there child, though she mid pretend to hate en, and say she wishes the baby and her too were in the church-yard," observed the woman in the red petticoat.

"She'll soon leave off saying that," replied the one in buff. "Lord, 'tis wonderful what a body can get used to o' that sort in time!"

"A little more than persuading had to do wi' the coming o't, I reckon. There were they that heard a sobbing one night last year in The Chase; and it mid ha' gone hard wi' a certain party if folks had come along."

"Well, a little more, or a little less, 'twas a thousand pities that it should have happened to she, of all others. But 'tis always the comeliest! The plain ones be as safe as churches—hey, Jenny?" The speaker turned to one of the group who certainly was not ill-defined as plain.

It was a thousand pities, indeed; it was impossible for even an enemy to feel otherwise on looking at Tess as she sat there, with her flower-like mouth and large tender eyes, neither black nor blue nor gray nor violet; rather all those shades together, and a hundred others, which could be seen if one looked into their irises—shade behind shade—tint beyond tint—around pupils that had no bottom; an almost standard woman, but for the slight incautiousness of character inherited from her race.

A resolution which had surprised herself had brought her into the fields this week for the first time during many months. After wearing and wasting her palpitating heart with every engine of regret that lonely inexperience could devise, common-sense had illumined her. She felt that she would do well to be useful again— to taste anew sweet independence at any price. The past was past; whatever it had been it was no more at hand. Whatever its consequences, time would close over them; they would all in a few years be as if they had never been, and she herself grassed down and forgotten. Meanwhile the trees were just as green as before; the birds sang and the sun shone as clearly now as ever. The familiar surroundings had not darkened because of her grief, nor sickened because of her pain.

She might have seen that what had bowed her head so profoundly—the thought of the world's concern at her situation—was founded on an illusion. She was not an existence, an experience, a passion, a structure of sensations, to anybody but herself. To all humankind besides Tess was only a passing thought. Even to friends she was no more than a frequently passing thought. If she made herself miserable the livelong night and day it was only this much to them—"Ah, she makes herself unhappy." If she tried to be cheerful, to dismiss all care, to take pleasure in the daylight, the flowers, the baby, she could only be this idea to them—"Ah, she bears it very well." Moreover, alone in a desert island would she have been wretched at what had happened to her? Not greatly. If she could have been but just created, to discover herself as a spouseless mother, with no experience of life except as the parent of a nameless child, would the position have caused her to despair? No, she would have taken it calmly, and found pleasures therein. Most of the misery had been generated by her conventional aspect, and not by her innate sensations.

Whatever Tess's reasoning, some spirit had induced her to dress herself up neatly as she had formerly done, and come out into the fields, harvest-hands being greatly in demand just then. This was why she had borne herself with dignity, and had looked people calmly in the face at times, even when holding the baby in her arms.

The harvest-men rose from the shock of corn, and stretched their limbs, and extinguished their pipes. The horses, which had been unharnessed and fed were again attached to the scarlet machine. Tess, having quickly eaten her own meal, beckoned to her eldest sister to come and take away the baby, fastened her dress, put on the buff gloves again and stooped anew to draw a bond from the last completed sheaf for the tying of the next.

In the afternoon and evening the proceedings of the morning were continued, Tess staying on till dusk with the body of harvesters. Then they all rode home in one of the largest wagons, in the company of a broad tarnished moon that had risen from the ground to the eastwards, its face resembling the outworn gold-leaf halo of some worm-eaten Tuscan saint. Tess's female companions sang songs, and showed themselves very sympathetic and glad at her reappearance out-of-doors, though they could not refrain from mischievously throwing in a few verses of the ballad about the maid who went to the merry green wood and came back a changed state. There are counterpoises and compensations in life; and the event which had made of her a social warning had also for the moment made her the most interesting personage in the village to many. Their friendliness won her still further away from herself, their lively spirits were contagious, and she became almost gay.

But now that her moral sorrows were passing away a fresh one arose on the natural side of her which knew no social law. When she reached home it was to learn to her grief that the baby had been suddenly taken ill since the afternoon. Some such collapse had been probable, so tender and puny was its frame; but the event came as a shock nevertheless.

The baby's offence against society in coming into the world was forgotten by the girl-mother; her soul's desire was to continue that offence by preserving the life of the child. However, it soon grew clear that the hour of emancipation for that little prisoner of the flesh was to arrive earlier than her worst misgivings had conjectured. And when she had discovered this she was plunged into a misery which transcended that of the child's simple loss. Her baby had not been baptized.

Tess had drifted into a frame of mind which accepted passively the consideration that if she should have to burn for what she had done, burn she must, and there was an end of it. Like all village girls, she was well grounded in the Holy Scriptures, and had dutifully studied the histories of Aholah and Aholibah, and knew the inferences to be drawn therefrom. But when the same question arose with regard to the baby, it had a very different colour. Her darling was about to die, and no salvation.

It was nearly bedtime, but she rushed downstairs and asked if she might send for the parson. The moment happened to be one at which her father's sense of the antique nobility of his family was highest, and his sensitiveness to the smudge which Tess had set upon that nobility most pronounced, for he had just returned from his weekly booze at Rolliver's Inn. No parson should come inside his door, he declared, prying into his affairs, just then, when, by her shame, it had become more necessary than ever to hide them. He locked the door and put the key in his pocket.

The household went to bed, and, distressed beyond measure, Tess retired also. She was continually waking as she lay, and in the middle of the night found that the baby was still worse. It was obviously dying—quietly and painlessly, but none the less surely.

In her misery she rocked herself upon the bed. The clock struck the solemn hour of one, that hour when fancy stalks outside reason, and malignant possibilities stand rock-firm as facts. She thought of the child consigned to the nethermost corner of hell, as its double doom for lack of baptism and lack of legitimacy; saw the arch-fiend tossing it with his three-pronged fork, like the one they used for heating the oven on baking days; to which picture she added many other quaint and curious details of torment sometimes taught the young in this Christian country. The lurid presentment so powerfully affected her imagination in the silence of the sleeping house that her nightgown became damp with perspiration, and the bedstead shook with each throb of her heart.

The infant's breathing grew more difficult, and the mother's mental tension increased. It was useless to devour the little thing with kisses; she could stay in bed no longer, and walked feverishly about the room.

"O merciful God, have pity; have pity upon my poor baby!" she cried. "Heap as much anger as you want to upon me, and welcome; but pity the child!"

She leant against the chest of drawers, and murmured incoherent supplications for a long while, till she suddenly started up.

"Ah! perhaps baby can be saved! Perhaps it will be just the same!"

She spoke so brightly that it seemed as though her face might have shone in the gloom surrounding her.

She lit a candle, and went to a second and a third bed under the wall, where she awoke her young sisters and brothers, all of whom occupied the same room. Pulling out the washing-stand so that she could get behind it, she poured some water from a jug, and made them kneel around, putting their hands together with fingers exactly vertical. While the children, scarcely awake, awe-stricken at her manner, their eyes growing larger and larger, remained in this position, she took the baby from her bed—a child's child—so immature as scarce to seem a sufficient personality to endow its producer with the maternal title. Tess then stood erect with the infant on her arm beside the basin, the next sister held the Prayer-Book open before her, as the clerk at church held it before the parson; and thus the girl set about baptizing her child.

Her figure looked singularly tall and imposing as she stood in her long white nightgown, a thick cable of twisted dark hair hanging straight down her back to her waist. The kindly dimness of the weak candle abstracted from her form and features the little blemishes which sunlight might have revealed—the stubble scratches upon her wrists, and the weariness of her eyes—her high enthusiasm having a transfiguring effect upon the face which had been her undoing, showing it as a thing of immaculate beauty, with a touch of dignity which was almost regal. The little ones kneeling round, their sleepy eyes blinking and red, awaited her preparations full of a suspended wonder which their physical heaviness at that hour would not allow to become active.

The most impressed of them said:

"Be you really going to christen him, Tess?"

The girl-mother replied in a grave affirmative.

"What's his name going to be?"

"SORROW, I baptize thee in the name of the Father, and of the Son, and of the Holy Ghost."

She sprinkled the water, and there was silence.

"Say 'Amen,' children."

The tiny voices piped in obedient response "Amen!"

Tess went on:

"We receive this child"—and so forth—"and do sign him with the sign of the Cross."

Here she dipped her hand into the basin, and fervently drew an immense cross upon the baby with her forefinger, continuing with the customary sentences as to his manfully fighting against sin, the world, and the devil, and being a faithful soldier and servant unto his life's end. She duly went on with the Lord's Prayer, the children lisping it after her in a thin, gnat-like wail, till, at the conclusion, raising their voices to clerk's pitch, they again piped into the silence, "Amen!"

Then their sister, with much augmented confidence in the efficacy of this sacrament, poured forth from the bottom of her heart the thanksgiving that follows, uttering it boldly and triumphantly in the stopt-diapason note which her voice acquired when her heart was in her speech, and which will never be forgotten by those who knew her. The ecstasy of faith almost apotheosized her; it set upon her face a glowing irradiation, and brought a red spot into the middle of each cheek; while the miniature candle-flame inverted in her eye-pupils shone like a diamond. The children gazed up at her with more and more reverence, and no longer had a will for questioning. She did not look like Sissy to them now, but as a being large, towering, and awful—a divine personage with whom they had nothing in common.

Poor Sorrow's campaign against sin, the world, and the devil was doomed to be of limited brilliancy—luckily perhaps for himself, considering his beginnings. In the blue of the morning that fragile soldier and servant breathed his last, and when the other children awoke they cried bitterly, and begged Sissy to have another pretty baby.

The calmness which had possessed Tess since the christening remained with her in the infant's loss. In the daylight, indeed, she felt her terrors about his soul to have been somewhat exaggerated; whether well founded or not she had no uneasiness now, reasoning that if Providence would not ratify such an act of approximation she, for one, did not value the kind of heaven lost by the irregularity—either for herself or for her child.

So passed away Sorrow the Undesired—that intrusive creature, that bastard gift of shameless Nature who respects not the social law; a waif to whom eternal Time had been a matter of days merely, who knew not that such things as years and centuries ever were; to whom the cottage interior was the universe, the week's weather climate, new-born babyhood human existence, and the instinct to suck human knowledge.

Tess, who mused on the christening a good deal, wondered if it were doctrinally sufficient to secure a Christian burial for the child. Nobody could tell this but the parson of the parish, and he was a newcomer, and did not know her. She went to his house after dusk, and stood by the gate, but could not summon courage to go in. The enterprise would have been abandoned if she had not by accident met him coming homeward as she turned away. In the gloom she did not mind speaking freely.

"I should like to ask you something, sir."

He expressed his willingness to listen, and she told the story of the baby's illness and the extemporized ordinance.

"And now, sir," she added earnestly, "can you tell me this— will it be just the same for him as if you had baptized him?"

Having the natural feelings of a tradesman at finding that a job he should have been called in for had been unskilfully botched by his customers among themselves, he was disposed to say no. Yet the dignity of the girl, the strange tenderness in her voice, combined to affect his nobler impulses—or rather those that he had left in him after ten years of endeavour to graft technical belief on actual scepticism. The man and the ecclesiastic fought within him, and the victory fell to the man.

"My dear girl," he said, "it will be just the same."

"Then will you give him a Christian burial?" she asked quickly.

The Vicar felt himself cornered. Hearing of the baby's illness, he had conscientiously gone to the house after nightfall to perform the rite, and, unaware that the refusal to admit him had come from Tess's father and not from Tess, he could not allow the plea of necessity for its irregular administration.

"Ah—that's another matter," he said.

"Another matter—why?" asked Tess, rather warmly.

"Well—I would willingly do so if only we two were concerned. But I must not—for certain reasons."

"Just for once, sir!"

"Really I must not."

"O sir!" She seized his hand as she spoke.

He withdrew it, shaking his head.

"Then I don't like you!" she burst out, "and I'll never come to your church no more!"

"Don't talk so rashly."

"Perhaps it will be just the same to him if you don't? . . . Will it be just the same? Don't for God's sake speak as saint to sinner, but as you yourself to me myself—poor me!"

How the Vicar reconciled his answer with the strict notions he supposed himself to hold on the subject it is beyond a layman's power to tell, though not to excuse. Somewhat moved, he said in this case also—

"It will be just the same."

So the baby was carried in a small deal box, under an ancient woman's shawl, to the churchyard that night, and buried by lantern-light, at the cost of a shilling and a pint of beer to the sexton, in that shabby corner of God's allotment where He let the nettles grow, and where all unbaptized infants, notorious drunkards, suicides, and others of the conjecturally damned were laid. In spite of the untoward surroundings, however, Tess bravely made a little cross of two laths and a piece of string, and having bound it with flowers, she stuck it up at the head of the grave one evening when she could enter the churchyard without being seen, putting at the foot also a bunch of the same flowers in a little jar of water to keep them alive. What matter was it that on the outside of the jar the eye of mere observation noted the words "Keelwell's Marmalade"? The eye of maternal affection did not see them in its vision of higher things.

From *Tess of the d'Urbervilles* by Thomas Hardy

Erma Bombeck

Possibly the greatest gift that Erma Bombeck (1927–   ), author and columnist, has is her ability to take everyday, energy-sapping happenings and clothe them with sufficient lightness and wit to make the daily grind endurable—and even sometimes enjoyable. She says with humor and touches of poignancy the things that her counterparts all over America are thinking and wishing they were clever enough to write down. Her writing is not only a catharsis for herself but for all other women in similar predicaments—"If Life Is a Bowl of Cherries, What Am I Doing in the Pits?"

Born in Dayton, Ohio, she began her newspaper career as a copy girl on the staff of the Dayton Journal Herald. *Then for a year she worked as a cub reporter before being assigned to the women's department for five years.*

She is married to William Bombeck, a retired educator, and they live in Arizona. They have two sons and one daughter who furnish the basis of much of her copy. Her thrice-weekly humor column, "At Wit's End," appears in more than 800 newspapers with a total circulation in excess of 40 million. In addition she makes regular appearances on ABC-TV's "Good Morning, America."

No one looks more like the ideal Mrs. America than she: blond, bubbling, warm, bright, impishly cherubic-looking. Erma Bombeck has elevated humor to an art and made laughter a therapy.

❋ EVERYTHING is in readiness.

The tree is trimmed. The cards taped to the doorframe. The boxes stacked in glittering disarray under the tree.

Why don't I hear chimes?

Remember the small boy who made the chimes ring in a fictional story years ago? As the legend went, the chimes would not ring unless a gift of love was placed on the altar. Kings and men of great wealth placed untold jewels on the altar, but year after year the church remained silent.

Then one Christmas Eve, a small child in a tattered coat made his way down the aisle and without anyone noticing he took off his coat and placed it on the altar. The chimes rang out joyously throughout the land to mark the unselfish giving of a small boy.

I used to hear chimes.

I heard them the year one of my sons gave me a tattered piece of construction paper on which he had crayoned two hands folded in prayer and a moving message, "OH COME HOLY SPIT!"

I heard them the year I got a shoebox that contained two baseball cards and the gum was still with them.

I heard them the Christmas they all got together and cleaned the garage.

They're gone, aren't they? The years of the lace doilies fashioned into snowflakes . . . the hands traced in plaster of paris . . . the Christmas trees of pipe cleaners . . . the thread spools that held small candles. They're gone.

The chubby hands that clumsily used up two dollars' worth of paper to wrap a cork coaster are sophisticated enough to take a number and have the gift wrapped professionally.

The childish decision of when to break the ceramic piggybank with a hammer to spring the fifty-nine cents is now resolved by a credit card.

The muted thump of pajama-covered feet paddling down the stairs to tuck her homemade crumb scrapers beneath the tree has given way to pantyhose and fashion boots to the knee.

It'll be a good Christmas. We'll eat too much. Make a mess in the living room. Throw the warranties into the fire by mistake. Drive the dog crazy taping bows to his tail. Return cookies to the plate with a bite out of them. Listen to Christmas music.

But Lord . . . what I would give to bend low and receive a gift of toothpicks and library paste and hear the chimes just one more time.

From *If Life Is a Bowl of Cherries—
What Am I Doing in the Pits?* by Erma Bombeck

Fanny Kemble

Fanny Kemble (1809–1893) was the youngest member of the Kemble family of actors which for three generations was renowned in Great Britain. Its more famous member, Sarah Kemble Siddons, Fanny's aunt, bore the family name for the first nineteen years of her life only. Fanny's father, Charles, was Sarah's brother.

At the age of nineteen, without experience, Fanny made her debut in 1829 as Juliet in an effort to save The Theatre Royal Covent Garden, London, from sale by its creditors. Her father was owner-actor-manager of Covent Garden. Fanny Kemble was immediately and immensely successful. In her first season she earned thirteen thousand pounds for the Theatre, thus paying off most of the pressing debts.

When she toured in America in 1832 she was enthusiastically received. Two years later she married Pierce Butler of Philadelphia and moved with him to a Georgia plantation. After fifteen years she was divorced from a husband who had expected her to swallow without protest slavery as well as his own shortcomings. She would not let him crush her integrity and wrote to a friend, "I cannot give my conscience into the keeping of another human being or submit the actions dictated by my conscience to his will."

Fanny Kemble was the last and least of the theatre Kembles. Writing, however, must also be considered one of her careers for she published plays, essays, one novel, and five journals. With these latter she earned lasting fame. Henry James declared that her journals "form together one of the most animated autobiographies in the language."

She was outspoken (she called this trait her "suddenness"), headstrong, tart, courageous, and casual about her fame. Those who disliked her did so rather vigorously. Thackery wrote, "Have learned to admire but not endure Mrs. Kemble." Yet as a young man he—and Tennyson—were in love with her when she first played Juliet. As she had her detractors so did she have her strong friends among whom were Browning, Scott, Longfellow, Mendelsohn, Henry James, and Liszt.

❋ IT was in the autumn of 1829, my father being absent on a professional tour in Ireland, that my mother, coming in from walking one day, threw herself into a chair and burst into tears. She had been evidently much depressed for some time past, and I was alarmed at her distress, of which I begged her to tell me the cause. "Oh, it has come at last," she answered: "our property is to be sold. I have seen that fine building all covered with placards and bills of sale; the theatre must be closed, and I know not how many hundred poor people will be turned adrift without employment." I believed the theatre employed regularly seven hundred persons in all its different departments, without reckoning the great number of what were called supernumeraries, who were hired by the night at Christmas, Easter, and on all occasions of any specially showy spectacle. Seized with a sort of terror like the Lady of Shallott, that "The curse had come upon me," I comforted my mother with expressions of pity and affection, and as soon as I left her, wrote a most urgent entreaty to my father that he would allow me to act for myself, and seek employment as a governess, so as to relieve him at once at least of the burden of my maintenance. I brought this letter to my mother and begged her permission to send it, to which she consented; but I afterward learned she wrote by the same post to my father requesting him not to give a positive answer to my·letter until his return to town. The next day she asked me whether I seriously thought I had any real talent for the stage. My schoolday triumphs in Racine's "Andromaque" were far enough behind me, and I could only answer, with as much perplexity as good faith, that I had not the slightest idea whether I had or not. She begged me to learn some part and say it to her that she might form some opinion of my power, and I chose Shakespeare's Portia, then as now my ideal of a perfect woman—the wise, witty woman, loving with all her soul and submitting with all her heart to a man whom everybody but herself (who was the best judge) would have judged her inferior: the laughter-loving, light-hearted, true-hearted, deep-hearted woman, full of keen perception, of active efficiency, of wisdom prompted by love, of tenderest unselfishness, of generous magnanimity; noble, simple, humble, pure; true, dutiful, religious, and full of fun; delightful above all others, the woman of women. Having learned it by heart, I recited Portia to my mother, whose only comment was, "There is hardly passion enough in this part to test any tragic power. I wish you would study Juliet for me." Study to me then, as unfortunately long afterward, simply meant to learn by heart, which I did again, and repeated my lesson to my mother, who again heard me without any observation whatever. Meantime my father returned to town and my letter remained unanswered, and I was wondering in my mind what reply I should receive to my urgent entreaty, when one morning my mother told me she wished me to recite Juliet to my father; and so in the evening I stood up before them both and with indescribable trepidation repeated my first lesson in tragedy.

They neither of them said anything beyond "Very well—very nice, my dear," with many kisses and caresses, from which I escaped to sit down on the stairs halfway between the drawing room and my bedroom and got rid of the repressed nervous fear I had struggled with while reciting in floods of tears. A few days after this my father told me he wished to take me to the theatre with him to try whether my voice was of sufficient strength to fill the building; so thither I went. That strange-looking place, the stage with its racks of pasteboard and canvas—streets, forest, banqueting halls, and dungeons—drawn apart on either side, was empty and silent; not a soul was stirring in the indistinct recesses of its mysterious depths, which seemed to stretch indefinitely behind me. In front, the great amphitheatre, equally empty and silent, wrapped in its gray holland covers, would have been absolutely dark but for a long sharp, thin shaft of light that darted here and there from some height and distance far above me and alighted in a sudden vivid spot of brightness on the stage. Set down in the midst of twilight space, as it were, with only my father's voice coming to me from where he stood hardly distinguishable in the gloom, in those poetical utterances of pathetic passion I was seized with the spirit of the thing; my voice resounded through the great vault above and before me, and completely carried away by the inspiration of the wonderful play, I acted Juliet as I do not believe I ever acted it again, for I had no visible Romeo, and no audience to thwart my imagination; at least I had no consciousness of any, though in truth I had one. In the back of one of the private boxes, commanding the stage but perfectly invisible to me, sat an old and warmly attached friend of my father's, Major D--------, a man of the world of London society, a passionate lover of the stage, an amateur actor of no mean merit, the best judge in many respects that my father could have selected, of my capacity for my profession and my chance of success in it. Not till after the event had justified my kind old friend's prophecy did I know that he had witnessed that morning's performance, and joining my father at the end of it had said, "Bring her out at once; it will be a great success." And so three weeks from that time I was brought out, and it was a "great success." Three weeks was not much time for preparation of any sort for such an experiment, but I had no more to become acquainted with my fellow actors and actresses, not one of whom I had ever spoken with or seen—off the stage—before; to learn all the technical business as it was called, of the stage; how to carry myself toward the audience, which was not—but was to be—before me; how to concert my movements with the movements of those I was acting with, so as not to impede or intercept their efforts, while giving the greatest effect of which I was capable to my own.

From *Fanny the American Kemble* by Fanny Kemble Wister

Becky Thatcher

In Mark Twain's The Adventures of Tom Sawyer *(1876) certain characters, in addition to Tom, always remain fresh: Aunt Polly, Huckleberry Finn, the Widow Douglas, Injun Joe, and, of course, Becky Thatcher.*

Tom falls in love with Becky the moment he sees her—"a lovely little blue-eyed creature with yellow hair plaited into two long tails, white summer frock, and embroidered pantalettes." And as he falls in love with Becky, he falls out of love with Amy Lawrence whom he had just spent months winning.

The romance is marked for a time by either one or the other's being piqued at the other. Different things, however, help to produce an upswing. Tom, with some friends, has been missing for some time. No one in the little town considers them runaways, so they are presumed dead and funeral services planned. Becky moans, "Oh, if I only had his brass andiron knob again! But I haven't got anything now to remember him by." The appearance of the boys at their own funeral turns the obsequies into rejoicing.

Later on, Tom becomes a hero in Becky's eyes. Accidentally, Becky has torn a page in one of the schoolmaster's books. To compound the offense, it is an anatomy book and the page is a picture of a nude figure. Tom comes along just as it happens, but perversely offers no sympathy. Both know what will happen. Mr. Dobbins, the schoolmaster, will question each pupil, and flog the student who did it. The interrogation begins. The master goes down the line. "Did you?" "Did you?" The next is Becky. "Rebecca Thatcher, did you tear this book?"

Tom springs to his feet and shouts, "I done it." And as he goes to sleep that night he thinks that Becky's adoration and gratitude are worth a hundred beatings. Her final words linger dreamily in his ear: "Tom, how could you be so noble!"

✻ WHEN school broke up at noon, Tom flew to Becky Thatcher, and whispered in her ear:

"Put on your bonnet and let on you're going home; and when you get to the corner, give the rest of 'em the slip, and turn down through the lane and come back. I'll go the other way, and come it over 'em the same way."

So the one went off with one group of scholars, and the other with another. In a little while the two met at the bottom of the lane, and when they reached the school they had it all to themselves. Then they sat together, with a slate before them, and Tom gave Becky the pencil and held her hand in his, guiding it, and so created another surprising house. When the interest in art began to wane, the two fell to talking. Tom was swimming in bliss. He said:

"Do you love rats?"

"No, I hate them!"

"Well, I do too—live ones. But I mean dead ones, to swing around your head with a string."

"No, I don't care for rats much, anyway. What *I* like is chewing gum!"

"Oh, I should say so! I wish I had some now!"

"Do you? I've got some. I'll let you chew it awhile, but you must give it back to me."

That was agreeable, so they chewed it turn about, and dangled their legs against the bench in excess of contentment.

"Was you ever at a circus?" said Tom.

"Yes, and my pa's going to take me again some time, if I'm good."

"I been to the circus three or four times—lots of times. Church ain't shucks to a circus. There's things going on at a circus all the time. I'm going to be a clown in a circus when I grow up."

"Oh, are you! That will be nice. They're so lovely all spotted up."

"Yes, that's so. And they get slathers of money—most a dollar a day, Ben Rogers says. Say, Becky, was you ever engaged?"

"What's that?"

"Why, engaged to be married."

"No."

"Would you like to?"

"I reckon so. I don't know. What is it like?"

"Like? Why, it ain't like anything. You only just tell a boy you won't ever have anybody but him, ever ever *ever*, and then you kiss, and that's all. Anybody can do it."

"Kiss? What do you kiss for?"

"Why that, you know, is to—well, they always do that."

"Everybody?"

"Why, yes, everybody that's in love with each other. Do you remember what I wrote on the slate?"

"Ye-yes."

"What was it?"

"I shan't tell you."

"Shall I tell *you?*"

"Ye-yes—but some other time."

"No, now."

"No, not now—to-morrow."

"Oh, no, *now,* please, Becky. I'll whisper it, I'll whisper it ever so easy."

Becky hesitating, Tom took silence for consent, and passed his arm about her waist and whispered the tale ever so softly, with his mouth close to her ear. And then he added:

"Now you whisper it to me—just the same."

She resisted for a while, and then said:

"You turn your face away, so you can't see, and then I will. But you mustn't ever tell anybody—*will* you, Tom? Now you won't—*will* you?"

"No, indeed indeed I won't. Now Becky."

He turned his face away. She bent timidly around till her breath stirred his curls, and whispered, "I—love—you!"

Then she sprang away and ran around and around the desks and benches, with Tom after her, and took refuge in a corner at last, with her little white apron to her face. Tom clasped her about her neck and pleaded.

"Now Becky, it's all over—all over but the kiss. Don't you be afraid of that—it ain't anything at all. Please, Becky."

And he tugged at the apron and the hands.

By and by she gave up and let her hands drop; her face, all glowing with the struggle, came up and submitted. Tom kissed the red lips and said:

"Now it's all done, Becky. And always after this, you know, you ain't ever to love anybody but me, and you ain't ever to marry anybody but me, never and for ever. Will you?"

"No, I'll never love anybody but you, Tom, and I'll never marry anybody but you, and you ain't to ever marry anybody but me, either."

"Certainly. Of course. That's *part* of it. And always, coming to school, or when we're going home, you're to walk with me, when there ain't anybody looking—and you choose me and I choose you at parties, because that's the way you do when you're engaged."

"It's so nice. I never heard of it before."

"Oh it's ever so jolly! Why me and Amy Lawrence—"

The big eyes told Tom his blunder, and he stopped, confused.

"Oh, Tom! Then I ain't the first you've ever been engaged to!"

The child began to cry. Tom said:

"Oh, don't cry, Becky. I don't care for her any more."

"Yes, you do, Tom—you know you do."

Tom tried to put his arm about her neck, but she pushed him away and turned her face to the wall, and went on crying. Tom tried again, with soothing words in his mouth, and was repulsed again. Then his pride was up, and he strode away and went outside. He stood about, restless and uneasy for a while, glancing at the door every now and then, hoping she would repent and come to find him. But she did not. Then he began to feel badly, and fear that he was in the wrong. It was a hard struggle with him to make new advances now, but he nerved himself to it and entered. She was still standing back there in the corner, sobbing with her face to the wall. Tom's heart smote him. He went to her and stood a moment, not knowing exactly how to proceed. Then he said, hesitatingly:

"Becky, I—I don't care for anybody but you."

No reply—but sobs.

"Becky?" pleadingly.

"Becky, won't you say something?"

More sobs.

Tom got out his chiefest jewel, a brass knob from the top of an andiron, and passed it around her so that she could see it, and said:

"Please, Becky, won't you take it?"

She struck it to the floor. Then Tom marched out of the house and over the hills and far away, to return to school no more that day. Presently Becky began to suspect. She ran to the door; he was not in sight; she flew around to the play-yard; he was not there. Then she called:

"Tom! Come back, Tom!"

She listened intently, but there was no answer. She had no companions but silence and loneliness. So she sat·down to cry again and upbraid herself, and by this time the scholars began to gather again, and she had to hide her grief and still her broken heart, and take up the cross of a long dreary aching afternoon, with none among the strangers about her to exchange sorrows with.

From *The Adventures of Tom Sawyer* by Mark Twain

Beatrice Lillie

Although Beatrice Lillie (1898–   ), toasted on two continents as the funniest woman in the world, is internationally known as a beloved British comedienne, she was born in Toronto, Canada (in the Irish section). Later the family moved to England.

Her father she described as "a fey and somewhat fancy-free Orangeman." Her mother was "majestically poised with a will of iron" and bent upon improving all of them. One of her firm goals was theatrical success for herself or one of her daughters. She used to tell them that they were distantly related to Bernard Shaw, although according to her daughter "she never mentioned the mileage." She would add, "My branch of the Shaw family didn't think too much of Bernard when he was a child."

Beatrice Lillie performed first in London in 1914, but not until 1924 in the United States. Her performances very much reflected herself—witty, sophisticated, vivacious, every (other) inch a lady. Her mother's advice had been, "Be natural. Be yourself. If you have talent, it will be discovered." And as Bea Lillie herself declared, "Off stage or on, I'm the same inside."

In 1920 she married Robert Peel, later to be Sir Robert Peel, at which time she became what she called "a Lady in my own wrong." She never gave up her career. It would have been impossible for her to have just been Mrs. or Lady Peel. Furthermore, they needed her money.

If her career in any way marred her marriage, in no way did it make her a less loving mother to their only child, Bobbie, who was killed in World War II.

❋ A PLACE I stayed away from one night was my old haunt, the Café de Paris. I'd promised to attend a party there, but Bobbie was home on leave, soon to ship out in a troopship for oceans unknown. Ordinary Seaman Peel had distinguished himself in training to the point where he'd been instructed to sit entrance examinations preliminary to taking an officer's course. I used to pray every night, and not only then, that he would pass, that he would be kept ashore for at least a few more months. It all seemed so quick.

But he failed, and I couldn't understand why. Now there was a full-blown war on, with Germans and Italians and, very soon, the Japanese to fight, and it wasn't going any better for us. I took what consolation there was to be found in the thought that I shouldn't be the only woman weeping to see her son set sail for unknown ends of the earth. A strange mood of foreboding overtook me. For the first time I strongly regretted giving permission for my only son to volunteer.

Before he sailed, not too surprisingly, Bobbie wanted to be married; my permission would be needed for that, too. I knew the girl, and, because of the spirit of wartime urgency that dominated the situation, I had some doubt about this being a lasting relationship. I needed time to think about it. On the night I was supposed to be at the Café de Paris, Bobbie and I argued long and hard. It got to be so late that I was ashamed to turn up at the party. That was the night the Café de Paris, which we all thought was as safe as an air-raid shelter, received a direct hit, and forty people died in the rubble. Who says one shouldn't be a fatalist?

Bobbie shipped out from Liverpool, a bachelor. Years later, I learned that he joined an R.N. draft of some 200 men, which embarked on January 10, 1942, in the converted troopship *Letitia,* joining a large troop convoy. After dodging German reconnaissance planes, they arrived at Freetown, South Africa, two weeks later. After another fortnight, the enlarged convoy rounded the Cape and was divided in two. The *Letitia* went to Durban, arriving on February 14 for a week's stay. Bobbie was then transferred to a troopship bound for Colombo, Ceylon, and he must have arrived there by early March.

South Africa was apparently a kind of paradise to these young men who had been raised in the Depression of the nineteen-thirties and who had just endured over two dark years of danger and privation in Britain. I am thankful that my son and so many others were able to enjoy, however briefly, a few happy days of what seemed a bit like peace.

At about the time Japan entered the war, Charles Cochran had asked me to do another show for him. I eventually agreed. Bobbie had been gone for months, by then, and for much of the time I'd heard nothing from him. I had no idea where he was; letters to and from an unknown warship could say little else but "I love you—keep safe. . . ."

I was in my room at the Midland Hotel, relaxing over a game of "I spy with my little eye" with a few cast members after the Tuesday evening performance, when Mumsie telephoned from London and read me the Admiralty telegram opened by her in my absence. It said: RESULT JAPANESE AIR RAID CO-LOMBO HARBOUR EARLY EASTER SUNDAY MORNING . . . REGRET TO INFORM YOU . . . SON BELIEVED MISSING. Those were the words. That's how they wrote it.

I thought, "What should I do?" I thought, "How can he be *missing?* Why don't they know? He has to be somewhere." I couldn't think what to do, but do you know what I really did? I put on some lipstick.

Then I called Cockie, and he came to see me. When I told him what I'd heard, he said, without a second thought, "We'll close the show tomorrow, for as long as you need."

"Oh no," I said. "Don't do that. That would be terrible. I'll play the show. There are so many other women, the cast, the audience. You can't do that."

Then I told him what I'd been telling myself, silently, all the time. "Anyway, it says he's believed missing. Just *missing.*"

I wrote a notice that my dresser, Daisy Flanagan, pinned up

on the board by the stage door: "I know how you all feel. Don't lets talk about it. Bless you. Now, let's get on with our work."

That's what we did. Nobody said a word to me. I went through two shows, our first Wednesday matinee, and the regular evening performance. Only once, in the middle of my new song, I came off and started to cry. "Get out of that, Lillie," I said. "There are worse things. Think of your son. Don't think of yourself. He isn't the only one. Neither are you." But he was: to me.

I was certain he would come back. He must be in a hospital somewhere, I said. Maybe he lost his memory. Bobbie's bound to turn up if I keep looking for him. *Missing* meant that he had to be found.

I was so bright and gay *in public*. There was no giving way that night or for the nights to come—hundreds and hundreds of them—because I existed with the knowledge that I'd find him again. That certainly lasted through all the run of *Big Top* and for months or maybe years after that.

You just go on. I did a lot of work in a lot of places, at home and overseas. I did my best to entertain the troops anywhere, at any time, at home and abroad. And I kept looking. I'd be on a stage someplace, it didn't matter where, and instead of thinking about what I was singing, the thought would be in my mind, "Supposing I look in the wings. What should I do if Bobbie's standing in the wings?" All kinds of things circled round in my head.

There were so many other women with missing sons. They wrote to me, and I often talked with them. "Don't worry," I used to say. "You may as well cheer up. You have to, you know, because—well, they're *missing*, and that doesn't mean they're killed. There still is hope. Get that into your head. Press on and hope and pray."

When I arrived back in London after the tryout road tour, I received another Admiralty telegram: PRESUMED DEAD . . .

but I didn't believe it. I kept looking, and I kept hoping, heavily encouraged by family and friends. In retrospect, the constant hoping and searching seems wrong, though, at the time, it sustained me.

From *Every Other Inch a Lady* by Beatrice Lillie

Saint Theresa of Lisieux

Saint Theresa of Lisieux (1873–1897), a French Carmelite nun, became one of the most widely loved saints in the Catholic Church. Her name originally was Theresa Martin; her name in the monastery was Theresa of the Child Jesus, a fitting name for one who was to make her mark by practicing her "little way," that is, by striving for goodness through performing even the most humble tasks as well as possible for the glory of God.

She was the youngest of five daughters, and was particularly close to her father whose pet name for her as she was growing up was "My little Queen." She was so young when she wished to enter the convent that special ecclesiastical permission had to be obtained. The permission, understandably, was not immediately given, but at the age of fifteen she was allowed to enter the Carmelite convent at Lisieux where her two older sisters were already nuns.

Her holiness so impressed her religious superior (who was, as well, her blood sister) that she asked her to write her spiritual autobiography. This has become one of the most widely read religious autobiographies. The excerpt below tells of her clothing day, that day upon which the novice dons the religious habit. For the cloistered Carmelite nun this habit is of rough brown wool—voluminous and heavy but rich in its symbolism.

❋ AND now my clothing day drew near. Contrary to all expectations, my Father had recovered from a second attack, and the Bishop fixed the ceremony for January 10. The time of waiting had been long indeed, but now what a beautiful feast! Nothing was wanting, not even snow.

Do you remember my telling you, dear Mother, how fond I am of snow? While I was still quite small, its whiteness entranced me. Why had I such a fancy for snow? Perhaps it was because, being a little winter flower, my eyes first saw the earth clad in its beautiful white mantle. So, on my clothing day, I wished to see it decked, like myself, in spotless white. The weather was so mild that it might have been spring, and I no longer dared hope for snow. The morning of the feast brought no change and I gave up my childish desire, as impossible to be realised. My Father came to meet me at the enclosure door, his eyes full of tears, and pressing me to his heart exclaimed: "Ah! here is my little Queen!" Then, giving me his arm, we made our solemn entry into the public Chapel. This was his day of triumph, his last feast on earth; now his sacrifice was complete, and his children belonged to God. Celine had already confided to him that later on she also wished to leave the world for the Carmel. On hearing this he was beside himself with joy: "Let us go before the Blessed Sacrament," he said, "and thank God for all the graces He has granted us and the honour He has paid me in choosing His Spouses from my household. God has indeed done me great honour in asking for my children. If I possessed anything better I would hasten to offer it to Him." That something better was himself, *"and God received him as a victim of holocaust; He tried him as gold in the furnace, and found him worthy of Himself."*

After the ceremony in the Chapel I re-entered the Convent and the Bishop intoned the *Te Deum*. One of the priests observed to him that this hymn of thanksgiving was only sung at professions, but, once begun, it was continued to the end. Was it not right that this feast should be complete, since in it all other joyful days were reunited?

The instant I set foot in the enclosure again my eyes fell on the statue of the Child Jesus smiling on me amid the flowers and lights; then, turning towards the quadrangle, I saw that, in spite of the mildness of the weather, it was covered with snow. What a delicate attention on the part of Jesus! Gratifying the least wish of His little Spouse, He even sent her this. Where is the creature so mighty that he can make one flake of it fall to please his beloved?

Everyone was amazed, and since then many people, hearing of my desire, have described this event as "the little miracle" of my clothing day, and thought it strange I should be so fond of snow.

From *Soeur Therese of Lisieux* edited by T. N. Taylor

Val

Val appears to be one of the strongest characters in The Women's Room *by Marilyn French. The novel, published in 1977, has been hailed as a manifesto of the Women's Movement. Certainly it is a book with which numbers of women identify. More than one woman has said to me that it accurately describes her life (and this may be its greatest sadness).*

The book, although it tells of courage, has to me more than ordinary sadness because it tells of people who do not experience lasting love between men and women and who have no concept of the richness of faith. This does not make it a less remarkable book, simply a more sorrowful book.

Its latter half focuses on a small group of women who are graduate students at Harvard, and who draw strength from one another. Val, at thirty-nine, is one of this group. Divorced after four years of marriage, she has a teenage daughter with whom she is very close and who is raped when she is a student at the University of Chicago. A friend says of Val, "Valerie isn't a person, she's an experience." One of her closest friends describes her thus: "And she was a happy person: she was one of the happiest people I ever knew. There was a wholeness in her. . . . She went breezing through, and even though she was sensitive and aware of what was going on around her most of the time, it rarely flapped her."

But the rape is something with which she cannot cope—or rather what follows it: the treatment of Chris by the police, by the assistant state's attorneys, by the judge. Val looks upon all of it as a fight for existence in a world of men, The Enemy.

After the court proceedings end and Chris and Val are back in Boston, Chris withdraws from everything and everyone except her mother. Her need for her mother appears almost psychotic. Val, recognizing what this could do to her daughter's well-being, sends her to a farm in the Berkshires, but without sufficient explanation, thus causing Chris to be further bruised. Val herself becomes what she calls "part of the lunatic fringe that gets the middle to move over a bit." And it is in a demonstration for a black woman who has apparently been unjustly sentenced for murder that Val is killed by police fire.

As for Chris—who knows?

❋ THE phone rang . . . she [Val] picked it up. So we all heard it, the voice on the other end. Because it screamed, it shrieked, it was a high, little girl voice, and it cried out: "MOMMY! MOMMY!"

"What is it, Chris?" Val said, her whole body taut. Her fingers, Mira noticed, were twisted together and white. But her voice was calm.

"MOMMY!" Chris's voice screamed. "I've been raped!"

It seems incredible now, looking back, that all of that could have been jumbled together the way it was. I am amazed that any of us survived it. But I guess the human race has survived worse. I know it has. The question is, at what cost? Because wounds do leave scars, and scar tissue has no feeling. That's what people forget when they train their sons to be "men" by injuring them. There is a price for survival.

Val spoke calmly to Chris. Quickly she got details, told her to lock her door, to hang up and call the police, and she, Val, would be waiting, would be standing by the phone, and Chris was to call her as soon as the police came, or before, as soon as she had stopped talking to them. Quickly, briskly, she spoke and Chris kept saying, "Yes. Okay. Yes, Mommy. I will." She sounded twelve.

Val hung up the phone. She was standing beside the wall, and she turned and laid her head against it. She just stood there. Everyone had heard; no one knew what to do. At last, Kyla went up and touched her arm.

"You want us to stay with you? Or do you want us to get out of here?"

"There's no reason for you to stay," Val said, still facing the wall.

Swiftly, silently, people stood to leave. It was not that they did not care. It was a sense of delicacy, of intrusion on some part of Val's life that was more private even than her sexual adventures, or an account of her menstrual cycle. They went over to her, they touched her lightly, they said good night.

"If there is anything I can do . . ." everyone said.

But of course, there wasn't. What can you do with grief but respect it? Only Bart and Ben and Mira stayed. Val stood by the wall. Mira made drinks for all of them. Val smoked. Bart got her a chair and sat her in it, and when the phone rang again, he picked it up, and Val gasped, as if she thought he was going to take the call, but he handed it to her, and then he brought her an ashtray. The voice on the other end was softer now, and they could not hear it. Eventually, Val hung up. The police had come to Chris's apartment. The boy who had raped her was gone. He had raped her a few doors away from her house, and she had somehow gotten home and called the only person she could think to call, who happened, Val said grimly, to be a thousand miles away. The police were taking her to the hospital. Val had the name written on the wall. She dialed Chicago information and got the number of the hospital.

"It's crazy, but I have to do something," she said, smoking nervously. "Someone has to look after her, even if it's at a distance."

They sat there until three. Val kept calling. She called the hospital, where they left her dangling so long that she hung up and called again. And again, and again. Finally they told her Chris was no longer there. The police had taken her down to the station. Val called the Chicago police. It took some time and many calls to find out what precinct Chris had been taken to, but she found it finally, and got through, and asked what was happening to her child.

They were not sure. They kept her dangling, but she held on. Eventually Chris came to the phone. Her voice sounded, Val said later, hysterical but controlled.

"Don't press charges," Val said.

Chris argued. The police wanted her to do it. She knew the name and address of the boy who had raped her. They had other charges against him and they wanted as they put it, to nail him.

"Don't do it," Val kept saying. "You don't know what it will cost you."

But Chris was oblivious. "They want me to, and I'm going to," she said and hung up.

Val sat stunned. "She doesn't know what she's doing," she said, still holding the receiver in her hand. The dial tone buzzed through the room. She stood up and dialed again, got the station again. The man who answered was annoyed now: Val was becoming an irritation. He told her to hang on. He did not return. She waited ten minutes, then hung up and dialed again. In time, someone answered. He did not seem to know what she was talking about.

"I'll see," he said. "Hold on."

She held on for a long time, and eventually he returned.

"Sorry, ma'am, but she's gone. They took her home."

Val thanked him, hung up, and sank back into her chair. Then she started up, fished in a cabinet for the phone book, and rifled through the Yellow Pages. She dialed an airline and made a reservation for the following morning. She turned to Mira.

"Do you think you could drive me to the airport?"

From *The Women's Room* by Marilyn French

Liv Ullmann

Liv Ullmann (1939–   ), outstanding Norwegian actress, has achieved an international reputation on the stage and in films. An international reputation is not easily earned. In addition to great gifts, one has to be a traveler with the strength of a Valkyrie; in one month, she says, she made three trips to Los Angeles while playing in Ibsen's Brand *at the Norwegian Theatre and beginning an American film in Sweden.*

She was born in a small hospital in Tokyo, and her mother remembers a Japanese nurse bending down to whisper apologetically: "I'm afraid it's a girl. Would you prefer to inform your husband yourself?" Although she was born in Tokyo, quite properly Ullmann refers to herself as the woman from Trondhjem.

In the selection below she mentions friends meeting in later life and observing the changes in one another. The theme of change in one's self holds a fascination for her, and she has written a book about herself called Changing. *She writes, "All the time I am trying to change myself."*

Toward the end of the book she asks, "What is change?" She follows this question with others. "What am I striving for? To become the best possible human being? Or the best artist? . . . What will I do with the change?"

✳ MAMMA contracted tuberculosis. Every Sunday Bitten and I went to the sanatorium and waved. She looked like a stranger, we thought. For the first time I became aware of her as a human being with a reality beyond that of being my mamma. I missed her during the six months she was away and put her picture under my pillow instead of Papa's. When she came back, she was much heavier and no longer as young. She had more time than before. And I less for her.

I was in love for the first time. Although I didn't hear bells ringing, as Mamma had promised me. But it was wonderful even so.

His name was Jens.

We didn't talk much, for we were both shy—silence was part of our relationship. Life pulsated around us differently than it had earlier. Our good-nights by the gate were tremendously important. The nearest we ever came to bells ringing. Mamma began standing at the window behind the curtains when she expected me home. We had to find other gates. He almost always wore rubber boots and was much taller than I. One day he told me that it was over. He could not spend all his youth with a virgin, he said. Somewhere he had read that it might be harmful for a developing man not to have sex. Besides, he was about to take his exams and go to the university. As a student he could not go around with a fifteen-year-old. He hoped I understood and wouldn't take it personally.

We both had red faces. I had never heard him speak that many consecutive sentences. I stood by a strange gate carrying my innocence with shame, as I watched a gangling youth walk out of my life.

For several months after this I loved James Stewart. He was the standby of my youth, uncomplicated, always there to love when needed. When, much later, I met him in person, I blushed furiously. As if he could guess the adventures the two of us shared in my dreams.

When there was an interval in the passions, I attended a sewing circle. We kept together for many years. Confidences whispered over a bottle of soda, which later was replaced by cocoa, then tea, and in the end by Coca-Cola with aspirin in it. Young girls on the threshold of life, who would meet by chance in the street many years later. Evaluating and curious, they would observe the changes in each other.

From *Changing* by Liv Ullmann

Pearl Buck

In her autobiography, Pearl S. Buck (1892–1973) says that she was brought up in two worlds, belonging as much to one as to the other: the world of her American missionary parents and the world of a vast and captivating China. Although born in the United States, Pearl Sydenstricker, when only a few months old, was taken to China by her parents.

Her life and her writings have been a blend of East and West. A graduate of Randolph-Macon Women's College and of Cornell, she was awarded the Pulitzer Prize for her novel, The Good Earth, *and in 1938 received the Nobel Prize for Literature.*

She married John Lossing Buck, an agricultural expert in China. Their first child showed signs of mental retardation so in 1925 she brought her to the United States for medical attention. In 1934 she left China permanently. The following year she divorced Buck, and bought a home in Bucks County, Pennsylvania. A year later, she married Richard Walsh, president of the John Day publishing firm.

In the late 1930s and early 1940s Pearl Buck's work increasingly reflected her concern about woman's role in the modern world. She began writing about the differences and characteristics of American women. Her premise: that American society tended to treat modern women as though they lived in medieval society. Well-educated, they were still denied opportunities consonant with their education. She divided women of her time into three groups: (1) talented women, most of whom are in the arts or sciences; (2) satisfied homemakers completely wrapped up in household duties and child rearing; and (3) gunpowder women, those who "have surplus time, energy, and ability which they do not know how to use." In her opinion these constituted by far the largest number.

❋ I REMEMBER so well the first time my little girl and I saw each other. It was a warm mild morning in March. A Chinese friend had brought me a pot of budding plum blossoms the day before, and a spray of them had opened. That was the first thing I saw when I came out of the ether. The next thing was my baby's face. The young Chinese nurse had wrapped her in a pink blanket and she held her up for me to see. Mine was a pretty baby, unusually so. Her features were clear, her eyes even then, it seemed to me, wise and calm. She looked at me and I at her with mutual comprehension and I laughed.

I remember I said to the nurse, "Doesn't she look very wise for her age?" She was then less than an hour old.

"She does indeed," the nurse declared. "And she is beautiful too. There is a special purpose for this child."

How often have I thought of those words! I thought of them proudly at first, as the child grew, always healthy, always good. I remember when she was two months old that an old friend saw her for the first time. The child had never seen a man with a black mustache before and she stared for a moment and then drew down her little mouth to weep, though some pride kept her from actual tears.

"Extraordinary," my friend said. "She knows already what is strange to her."

I remember when she was only a month older that she lay in her little basket upon the sun deck of a ship. I had taken her there for the morning air as we traveled. The people who promenaded upon the deck stopped often to look at her, and my pride grew as they spoke of her unusual beauty and of the intelligence of her deep blue eyes.

I do not know where or at what moment the growth of her intelligence stopped, nor to this day do we know why it did. There was nothing in my family to make me fear that my child might be one of those who do not grow.

My little daughter's body continued its healthy progress. We had left North China by then, and were living in Nanking, which, next to Peking, perhaps, is China's richest city in history and humanity. Though my home was inside the city walls, it was still country living. Our house was surrounded by lawn and gardens, a bamboo grove and great trees. When the city walls were built, centuries ago, enough land was enclosed so that if the city were besieged, the people would not starve. Our compound was surrounded by farms and fish ponds.

It was a pleasant and healthy home for a child. She was still beautiful, as she would be to this day were the light of the mind behind her features. I think I was the last to perceive that something was wrong. She was my first child, and I had no close comparison to make with others. She was three years old when I first began to wonder.

For at three she did not yet talk. Now that my adopted babies have taught me so much, I realize that speech comes as naturally to the normal child as breathing. He does not need to be taught to talk—he talks as he grows. He hears words without knowing it and day by day increases the means of conveying his widening thoughts. Still, I became uneasy. In the midst of my pleasant surroundings, in all the fresh interest of a new period in Chinese history when the Nationalist government was setting itself up with such promise, I found life exciting and good. Yet I can remember my growing uneasiness about my child. She looked so well, her cheeks pink, her hair straight and blond, her eyes the clear blue of health. Why then the speech delay!

I remember asking friends about their children, and voicing my new anxiety about my child. Their replies were comforting, too comforting. They told me that children talked at different ages, that a child growing up in the house with other children learned more quickly than an only child. They spoke all the empty words of assurance that friends, meaning well, will use and I believed them. Afterward, when I knew the whole tragic truth, I asked them if they had no knowledge then of what had befallen my child. I found that they did have, that they had guessed and surmised and that the older ones even knew, but that they shrank from telling me.

To this day I cannot understand their shrinking. For to me truth is so much dearer than any comforting falsehood, so much kinder in its clean-cutting edge than fencing and evasion, that the better a friend is the more he must use truth. There is value in the quick and necessary wound. Thus my child was nearly four years old before I discovered for myself that her mind had stopped growing. To all of us there comes the hour of awakening to sad truth. Sometimes the whole awakening comes at once and in a moment. To others, like myself, it came in parts slowly. I was reluctant and unbelieving until the last.

It began one summer at a seashore in China, where the waves come in gently even in time of storm. It had been a mild and pleasant summer, shore set against mountains. I spent the mornings with my child on the beach and in the afternoons sometimes we went riding along the valleys on the small gray donkeys which stood for hire at the edge of the beach.

The child had now begun to talk, only a little, but still enough to quiet my fears for the moment. It must be remembered that I was wholly inexperienced in such children. Now my eyes can find in any crowd the child like mine. I see him first of all and then I see the mother, trying to smile, trying to speak to the child gaily, her gaiety a screen to hide him from the others. But then I did not see even my own child as she really was, I read meaning into her gestures and into the few broken words. "She doesn't talk because she gets everything she wants without it," a friend complained. So I tried to teach my child to ask for a thing first. She seemed not to understand.

I must have been more anxious than I knew, however, for I remember I went one day to hear an American visiting pediatrician give a lecture on the preschool child, and as I listened to her I realized that something was very wrong indeed with my child.

The doctor pointed out signs of danger which I had not understood. The slowness to walk, the slowness to talk, and then when the child could walk, the incessant restlessness which took the form of constant running hither and thither, were all danger signs. What I had taken to be the vitality of a splendid body I saw now might be the superenergy of a mind that had not kept control of the body.

After the meeting was over, I remember, I asked the doctor to come and see my child. She promised to come the next day. I told no one of my growing fear and through that sleepless night I went over and over in my mind all the good signs, the things the child could do: that she could feed herself; that she could put on her clothes, though not fasten buttons; that she liked to look at picture books; that she understood so much more than she could say. But I did not want false comfort. I wanted now and quickly the whole truth.

The doctor came the next day and sat a long time watching my child, and then she shook her head. "Something is wrong," she said, "I do not know what it is. You must have a consultation of doctors. Let them tell you, if they know."

She pointed out to me the danger signs I had not seen, or would not see. The child's span of attention was very short indeed, far shorter than it should have been at her age. Much of her fleet light running had no purpose—it was merely motion. Her eyes, so pure in their blue, were blank when one gazed into their depths. They did not hold or respond. They were changeless. Something was very wrong.

I thanked her and she went away. Thinking it over, I saw there was no reason why a stranger should stay to tell me more. Perhaps she knew no more. There is no task more difficult than to tell a parent that the beloved child will never grow to be an adult. I have done it sometimes since, and I have not allowed myself to shrink from it, but it has been hard. The heart can break more than once.

The doctors met the next day. I can still see the scene as though it took place before my eyes now. The house had a wide veranda, facing the sea. It was a glorious morning, and the sea was violet blue and calm except for the gentle white surf at the coast. The child had been with her Chinese nurse playing on the sand and wading in the water. I called and they came up the path between the bamboos. In spite of my terror, I was proud of my child as she stood before the doctors. She had on a little white swimming suit and her firm sun-browned body was strong and beautiful. In one hand she held her pail and shovel and in the other a white shell.

"She looks well enough," one of the doctors murmured.

Then they began to ask questions. I answered them with all the honesty I had. Nothing but honesty would do now. As they listened they watched and they began to see. The shell dropped from her hand and she did not pick it up. Her head drooped. The oldest doctor, who had known my parents, lifted her to his knee and began to test her reflexes. They were weak—almost non-existent.

The doctors were kind men and I begged them to tell me what they thought and then tell me what to do. I think they were honest in their wish to do this. But they did not know what was wrong or, whatever was wrong, how to cure it. I sat in silence and watched the child. I began to feel that they were agreed that development had stopped in the child, but they did not know why. There were so few physical symptoms—only the ones I have mentioned. They plied me with questions about the child's past, about her illnesses: had she ever had a high temperature, had she ever had a fall? There had been nothing. She had been sound from her birth and so cared for that she had never been hurt.

"You must take her to America," they told me at last. "There the doctors may know what is wrong. We can only say there is something wrong."

Then began that long journey which parents of such children know so well. I have talked with many of them since and it is always the same. Driven by the conviction that there must be someone who can cure, we take our children over the surface of the whole earth, seeking the one who can heal. We spend all the money we have and we borrow until there is no one else to lend. We go to doctors good and bad, to anyone, for only a wisp of hope. We are gouged by unscrupulous men who make money from our terror, but now and again we meet those saints who, seeing the terror and guessing the empty purse, will take nothing for their advice, since they cannot heal.

So I came and went, too, over the surface of the earth, gradually losing hope and yet never quite losing it, for no doctor said firmly that the child could never be healed. There were always the last hesitant words, "I don't want to say it is hopeless"; and so I kept hoping, in the way parents have.

It was getting harder all the time for another reason. The child was older and bigger and her broken speech and babyish ways were conspicuous. I had no sense of shame for myself. I had grown up among the Chinese, who take any human infirmity for what it is. Blind people, the lame, the halt, the tongue-tied, the deformed—during my life in China I had seen that all came and went among others and were accepted for themselves. Their infirmities were not ignored. Sometimes they were even made the cause of nicknames.

For example, Little Cripple was a playmate of my own early childhood, a boy with a twisted leg. According to our western notions, it would have been cruel to call him by his deformity. But the Chinese did not mean it so. That was the way he was, literally, and his twisted leg was part of himself. There was some sort of catharsis even for the boy in this taking for granted an affliction. Somehow it was easier than the careful ignoring of my American friends. The sufferer did not feel any need to hide himself. There he was, as he was, and everybody knew him. It was better than any sweet pretending that he was like everybody else.

More than this, the Chinese believed that since Heaven ordains, it was a person's fate to be whatever he was, and it was neither his fault nor his family's. They believed, too, with a sort of human tenderness, that if a person were handicapped in one way, there were compensations, also provided by Heaven. Thus a blind person was always treated with respect and even sometimes with fear, for it was thought he had a perception far beyond mere seeing.

All the years my child and I had lived among the Chinese we had breathed this frank atmosphere. My Chinese friends discussed my child with me easily as they discussed their own. But they were not experienced enough to know what was wrong or even that it was wrong. "The eyes of her wisdom are not yet opened," was the way they put it. "For some persons wisdom comes early and for others late—be patient." This was what they told me. When we walked on the narrow winding streets of our old city no one noticed when she stopped reasonlessly to clap her hands or if, without reason, she began to dance. Yes, the Chinese were kind to my child and to me. If they did notice her, it was only to smile at what they took to be her pleasure, and they laughed with her.

It was on the streets of Shanghai that I first learned that people were not all so kind. Two young American women walked along the street, newcomers from my own country, I supposed, by their smart garments. They stared at my child and when we had passed one of them said to the other, "The kid is nuts." It was the first time I had ever heard the slang phrase and I did not know what it meant. I had to ask someone before I knew. Truth can be put into brutal words. From that day I began to shield my child.

There is no use in giving the details of the long, sorrowful journey. We crossed the sea and we went everywhere, to child clinics, to gland specialists, to psychologists. I know now that it was all no use. There was no hope from the first—there never had been any. I do not blame those men and women for not telling me so—not altogether. I suppose some of them knew, but perhaps they didn't. At any rate, the end of each conference was to send us on to someone else, perhaps a thousand miles away.

The end of the journey for my child and me came one winter's day in Rochester, Minnesota. We had been sent finally to the Mayo Clinic, and day after day we had spent in the endless and meticulous detail of complete examination. My confidence had grown as the process went on. Surely so much study, so much knowledge, would tell me the truth and what to do with it.

We went at last into the office of the head of the children's department. It was evening and almost everybody had gone home. The big building was silent and empty. Outside the window I saw only darkness. My little girl was very tired and I remember she leaned her head against me and began to cry silently, and I took her upon my lap and held her close while I listened. The doctor was kind and good. I can see him still, a tall, rather young man, his eyes gentle and his manner slow as though he did not want anyone to be hurried or anxious. He held in his hand the reports sent in from all the departments where my child had been examined, and he made his diagnosis. Much of it was good. All the physical parts were excellent. My child had been born with a fine body.

There were other things good too. She had certain remarkable abilities, especially in music. There were signs of an unusual personality struggling against some sort of handicap. But—the mind was severely retarded.

I asked the question that I asked now every day of my life: "Why?"

He shook his head. "I don't know. Somewhere along the way, before birth or after, growth stopped."

He did not hurry me, and I sat on, still holding the child. Any parent who has been through such an hour knows that monstrous ache of the heart which becomes physical and permeates muscle and bone.

"Is it hopeless?" I asked him.

Kind man, he could not bear to say that it was. Perhaps he was not really sure. At least he would not say he was sure. "I think I would not give up trying," was what he finally said.

That was all. He was anxious to get home and there was no more reason to stay. He had done all he could. So again my child and I went out of the doctor's office and walked down the wide empty hall. The day was over and I had to think what to do next.

Now came the moment for which I shall be grateful as long as I live. I suppose to be told that my child could be well would have meant a gratitude still higher; but that being impossible, I have to thank a man who came quietly out of an empty room as I passed. He was a small, inconspicuous person, spectacled, a German by looks and accent. I had seen him in the head doctor's office once or twice. He had, in fact, brought in the sheaf of reports and then had gone away without speaking. I had seen him but without attention, although now I recognized him.

He came out almost stealthily and beckoned to me to follow him into the empty room. I went in, half bewildered, my child clinging to my hand. He began to speak quickly in his broken English, his voice almost harsh, his eyes sternly upon mine.

"Did he tell you the child might be cured?" he demanded.

"He—he didn't say she could not," I stammered.

"Listen to what I tell you!" he commanded. "I tell you, madame, the child can never be normal. Do not deceive yourself. You will wear out your life and beggar your family unless you give up hope and face the truth. She will never be well—do you hear me? I know—I have seen these children. Americans are all too soft. I am not soft. It is better to be hard, so that you can know what to do. This child will be a burden on you all your life. Get ready to bear that burden. She will never be able to speak properly. She will never be able to read or write, she will never be more than about four years old, at best. Prepare yourself, madame! Above all, do not let her absorb you. Find a place where she can be happy and leave her there and live your own life. I tell you the truth for your own sake. "

I can remember these words exactly as he spoke them. I suppose the shock photographed them upon my memory. I remember, too, exactly how he looked, a little man, shorter than I, his face pale. A small, clipped black mustache, under which his lips were grim. He looked cruel, but I know he was not. I know now that he suffered while he spoke. He believed in the truth.

I don't know what I said or even if I said anything. I remember walking down the endless hall again alone with the child. I cannot describe my feelings. Anyone who has been through such moments will know, and those who have not cannot know, whatever words I might use. Perhaps the best way to put it is that I felt as though I were bleeding inwardly and desperately. The child, glad to be free, began capering and dancing, and when she saw my face twisted with weeping, she laughed.

It was all a long time ago and yet it will never be over as long as I live. That hour is with me still.

I did not stop trying, of course, in spite of what the little German had said, but I think I knew in my heart from that moment on that he was right and that there was no hope. I was able to accept the final verdict when it came because I had already accepted it before, though unconsciously, and I took my child home again to China. I shall forever be grateful to him, whose name I do not even know. He cut the wound deep, but it was clean and quick. I was brought at once face to face with the inevitable.

From *The Child Who Never Grew* by Pearl Buck

Susan Dunne

Alice Duer Miller's long narrative poem, The White Cliffs, *published in 1940, was one of World War II's most romantic and cherished pieces of literature, but it was a World War I love-story. American college-age girls read it, loved it, listened to Lynn Fontanne's recording of it, memorized lines from it, and strongly identified with its American heroine, Susan Dunne, who at a ball in Belgrave Square falls in love with an Englishman. This greatly dismays her New England father who, from Rhode Island, writes, "You've fallen in love with an Englishman. Well, they're a manly, attractive lot, if you happen to like them, which I do not."*

But Susan marries her Englishman, Johnnie, and when he goes to France to fight, she settles down in Devon in the red brick manor house of his family with her mother-in-law—"two lonely women." Two lonely women, heroic in their endurance, their acceptance of war-time privation and eventually of the loss of those they love: first Percy, John's brother, and then John himself at Douai.

The White Cliffs *ends with the beginning of the Second World War when Susan has to accept her only son's willingness to die, like his father, for England. The poem, written before America had entered the war, was not without propaganda value. Its final lines are uttered by Susan, " . . . in a world where England is finished and dead, I do not wish to live."*

Susan's joy at her son's birth has a universal quality.

❋   Out of the dark, and dearth
       Of happiness on earth,
       Out of a world inured to death and pain;
       On a fair spring morn
       To me a son was born,
       And hope was born—the future lived again.

To me a son was born,
The lonely hard forlorn
Travail was, as the Bible tells, forgot.
How old, how commonplace
To look upon the face
Of your first-born, and glory in your lot.

To look upon his face,
And understand your place
Among the unknown dead in churchyards lying
To see the reason why
You lived and why you die—
Even to find a certain grace in dying.

To know the reason why
Buds blow, and blossoms die,
Why beauty fades, and genius is undone,
And how unjustified
Is any human pride
In all creation—save in this common one.

Maternity is common, but not so
It seemed to me. Motherless, I did not know—
I was all unprepared to feel this glow,
Holy as a Madonna's, and as crude
As any animal's beatitude—
Crude as my own black cat's, who used to bring
Her newest litter to me every spring,
And say, with green eyes shining in the sun:
"Behold this miracle that I have done."

And John came home on leave, and all was joy
And thankfulness to me, because my boy
Was not a baby only, but the heir—
Heir to the Devon acres and a name

As old as England. Somehow I became
Almost an English woman, almost at one
With all they did—all they had done.

From *The White Cliffs*
by Alice Duer Miller

Caitlin Thomas

Caitlin Thomas (1913–   ) is the widow of the Welsh poet, Dylan Thomas. For her, Dylan and dying could not go together, yet they were bound to go together. Dylan Thomas lived recklessly and drank heavily. His death, before he was forty, was brought on by alcoholism.

In her memoir she tells of the time leading up to his death, and her self-exile for a period to Elba with her youngest son, Colm. Elizabeth Bowen writes that this work showed "the savagery of total loss." Was the time in Italy more healing than Caitlin thought? At the least, it got her away from Wales and "the old Dylan-infested life." But when she left the island to return home she wrote as the final sentence, "And all the king's horses, and all the king's men, couldn't put Caitlin Thomas together again."

During her time on the island she often neglected Colm, her child (in part because, as she writes, she "was guilty of loving a young boy"). She saw to it that Colm was fed, clothed, washed, but admittedly gave him none of the concentrated personal attention important to a child. Not so, however, when mother and son first arrived. Sending him off to school left her with all the traditional fears of a mother facing this first separation.

❋ ONE formidable step I at last took, with agonized pushing and trepidation; sent Colm to school. Had I sent him to the guillotine, I couldn't have suffered more: but, after a lot of fuss, terror at them staring at him, he had felt it too, talking gibberish to him, and fantastic bribes on my part: I got him there. It was not quite so torturous as I feared: a darling smiling Sister, I was converted there and then; and a row of dazzling, ribbon-crisp, spick and span, pink check-pinafored small boys. Instead of leaving Colm, hanging about disconsolately in the background, as though he were nothing to do with *them*, as they mostly do in my experience, my beautiful Sister took him by the hand, led him to the front of the class, and presented him by name, explaining that he was English, and asking them to be nice to him.

He was received with cries of joy and clapping, and I could see that his reception pleased him immensely. I sent up a silent prayer of gratitude, and crept back, still screwed up in knots of tension, to sit among the debris of the night.

· ·

One day, for no special reason that I can remember, I suddenly felt whole again; and God, what a change. I was a new person, somebody I had forgotten a long time ago; I wanted to sing, and jump, and hug everybody, and kiss them. But it only lasted a day, then the wind came again and sent me shivering back where I had come from.

All this time Colm had been going to his asylum (*asilo*, as they not very encouragingly call the infant convent school), and I had taken one further perilous step, by leaving him there to lunch, which meant just soup; except that Italian soup is not quite the same as Windsor Brown; with extras supplemented by the mother. On the first day I went to great pains to get him the correct little cardboard case, tin plate, cup and spoon; and put in all the bits and pieces he liked best, including his special bananas; only to find, when I went to collect him later, he had been given the wrong case, full of cheeses and stuff he would not eat; and nearly broke his heart, watching the other boy eating his bananas. It nearly broke mine too; the baffling bewilderments of children, when they are transplanted from one familiar environment, to a frightening strange one, without knowing why; or worse still, the callous initiation into boarding school, which, to me, was the cruellest suffering; have the same quality of poignant unbearableness, as blinding cicadas to make them sing, clipping the wings of birds, tying cans to dogs' tails, leading cats on strings, tripping up cripples, tying goats' legs together, emptying nests of eggs, strewing the fledglings, caging any wild thing. And Colm, with his fair curls, novitiate's round white collar, and buttoned-tight-down-the-back black check tunic; with his stumpy trousered and booted legs coming out below, looked such a story-book angel of innocence, among the sloe-eyed, crafty by comparison, already mature natives. But this did not prevent me afterwards from half-killing him for some act of unmitigated fiendery, far more imaginative than anything the naive darkies could have dreamed of perpetrating.

At nights we clung together, like the white haired, ship-wrecked, ancient mariner and son; and this scrap of Dylan contact was both comforting and disturbing to me. With all Colm's demands and disturbances, I did thank thankless God, because there was nobody else to thank, he was there. He kept me on the move, tied me to certain times; and most of all, gave me a chance to meet the people, whom otherwise I would have had no excuse to talk to. Without him I am sure I would have walked straight over the nearest mountain, into an impenetrable mist, like Oates in the Antarctic, and never been seen again.

From *Leftover Life to Kill* by Caitlin Thomas

Eleanor Roosevelt

Eleanor Roosevelt (1884–1962) was the niece of one President,
Theodore, and the wife of another, Franklin. Her tireless dedi-
cation to the cause of human welfare won her affection and honor
throughout the world, but her children, according to one of her
sons, always felt closer to their father. As a mother her life was
made particularly difficult by the continuous, autocratic interfer-
ence of her mother-in-law in the upbringing of her children. On
the other hand, she herself was often too much of a disciplinarian
with them, possibly a reflection of her own austere upbringing.

She may have been one of those persons able to show warmth
and love more easily in letters. Certainly the following letter to
her only daughter, Anna, is filled with loving disappointment.

 Christmas Eve, 1935

Darling Anna,

Perhaps I needed to have you away this Xmas to realize just
how much it means to have you, and so I think I'll try to tell you
in these few minutes before dinner how much I miss you. The
dogs and I have felt sad every time we passed your door. It was
hard to decorate the tree or get things distributed at the afternoon
party without you and I dread dinner tomorrow night for so many
of your friends will miss you and if anyone says much I shall
weep for I've had a queer feeling in my throat whenever I thought
of you. Anyway I am happy that you and John are together for
I know you will be happy. So please give him a hug for me and
tell him I am grateful for him and for what he means to you every
day of my life. . . . When I go to church tonight I'll pray for

long life and happiness for each and every one of you who mean so much to me and may I always realize what a blessed person you are dearest one.

Mother

From *A Love in Shadow* by John R. Bocttiger

Golda Meir

Golda Meir (1898–1979), the school teacher (in Milwaukee) who became Prime Minister of Israel, spent the first eight years of her life in Russia. From there, crossing the border secretly with her family, she came to the United States. What she called "A New Life" was not, however, to begin until she went to Palestine.

In Palestine she became active in both the labor movement and the struggle against the British. After Israeli independence her first important post was as minister to Russia, then minister of labor, and foreign minister. Upon the death (1969) of Levi Eshkol she became interim Prime Minister and retained the post in the election.

In her autobiography she discusses many moving moments in her life, among which were the reading to the new nation of the proclamation of independence by Ben-Gurion in the Tel Aviv museum and the request to serve at the time of Eshkol's death as interim Prime Minister.

Another experience that she looked upon as one of the most moving she describes in My Life *. The incident, involving a soldier, took place two years before she became Prime Minister. It could just as easily have happened after her election.*

❋ ONE evening, however, I went to the Western Wall—not for the first time. Morris and I had gone there a week or two after our arrival in Palestine. I had grown up in a Jewish home, a good traditional Jewish home, but I wasn't at all pious, and truth is that I went to the Wall without much emotion, just as something that I knew I ought to do. Then, all of a sudden, at the end of those narrow, winding alleys in the Old City, I saw it. The Wall itself looked much smaller than it does today, after all the excavations. But for the first time I saw the Jews, men and women, praying and weeping before it and putting *kvitlach*—their scribbled petitions to the Almighty—into its crannies. So this was what was left of a past glory, I thought, all that has remained of Solomon's Temple. But at least it was still there. And in those Orthodox Jews with their *kvitlach,* I saw a nation's refusal to accept that only these stones were left to it and an expression of confidence in what was to come in the future. I left the Wall changed in feeling—uplifted is perhaps the word. And on that evening, years later, when I was so dissatisfied with everything, the Wall still had a message for me.

In 1971 I was awarded the Freedom of Jerusalem—probably the greatest tribute ever paid me—and at that ceremony I told of yet another memorable visit I had made to the Wall, this time in 1967, after the Six-Day War. For nineteen years, from 1949 to 1967, we were banned by the Arabs from going to the Old City or praying at the Wall. But on the third day of the Six-Day War— Wednesday, June 7—all Israel was electrified by the news that our soldiers had liberated the Old City and that it was open to us again. I had to fly to the United States three days later, but I couldn't bring myself to leave Israel without going to the Wall again. So that Friday morning—although civilians were not yet allowed to enter the Old City because shooting was still going on there—I received permission to go to the Wall, despite the fact that I wasn't in the government then but just an ordinary citizen, like any other.

I went to the Wall together with some soldiers. There in front of it stood a plain wooden table with some submachine guns on it. Uniformed paratroopers wrapped in prayer shawls clung so tightly to the wall that it seemed impossible to separate them from it. They and the Wall were one. Only a few hours earlier they had fought furiously for the liberation of Jerusalem and had seen their comrades fall for its sake. Now, standing before the Wall, they wrapped themselves in prayer shawls and wept, and I, too, took a sheet of paper, wrote *"shalom"* (peace) on it and pushed it into a cranny of the Wall, as I had seen the Jews do so long ago. As I stood there, one of the soldiers (I doubt that he knew who I was) suddenly put his arms around me, laid his head on my shoulder, and we cried together. I suppose he needed the release and the comfort of an old woman's warmth, and for me it was one of the most moving moments of my life.

From *My Life* by Golda Meir

Charlotte Brontë

The short life of Charlotte Brontë (1816–1855), English novelist, was marked by deep familial love and deep sorrow, the two understandably intertwined. Although originally there were six Brontë children, five girls and one boy, it is Charlotte, Emily, and Anne who became well-known as English novelists. All six were to die before they were forty.

The woman who nursed their mother in her final illness said of the children, "I used to think of them as spiritless, they were so different to any children I had ever seen." She also, however, admitted, "But there never were such good children." It was on their beloved moors, wild and glorious, that the children found their release, just as later three of them were to find it in their writings, also, often wild and glorious.

At first the sisters kept their writings secret from one another. When Charlotte came upon Emily's poetry in 1845 then Anne revealed hers. Sharing resulted and the next year a collection of verse by the three appeared under the pseudonyms of Currer, Ellis, and Acton Bell. Their novels at first were published without their identity being known even to their publishers. It was not until 1849 that their identities became known, and by then for Emily it was too late. Her novel Wuthering Heights *was published in 1847. In September of the following year she caught cold at her brother's funeral and refusing until the morning of her death all medical aid died of tuberculosis the following December.*

In a letter that is possibly one of the more beautiful in the English language, Charlotte writes to tell a friend of Emily's death.

                                    Dec. 21st, 1848

EMILY suffers no more from pain or weakness now. She never will suffer more in this world. She is gone, after a hard, short conflict. She died on *Tuesday*, the very day I wrote to you. I thought it very possible she might be with us still for weeks; and a few hours afterwards, she was in eternity. Yes; there is no Emily in time or on earth now. Yesterday we put her poor, wasted, mortal frame quietly under the church pavement. We are very calm at present. Why should we be otherwise? The anguish of seeing her suffer is over; the spectacle of the pains of death is gone by; the funeral day is past. We feel she is at peace. No need now to tremble for the hard frost and the keen wind. Emily does not feel them. She died in a time of promise. We saw her taken from life in its prime. But it is God's will, and the place where she is gone is better than that she has left.

God has sustained me, in a way that I marvel at, through such agony as I had not conceived. I now look at Anne, and wish she were well and strong; but she is neither, nor is Papa. Could you now come to us for a few days? I would not ask you to stay long. Write and tell me if you could come next week, and by what train. I would try and send a gig for you to Keighley. You will, I trust, find us tranquil. Try to come. I never so much needed the consolation of a friend's presence. Pleasure, of course, there would be none for you in the visit, except what your kind heart would teach you to find in doing good to others."

From *The Life of Charlotte Brontë* by E. C. Gaskell

Mary McCarthy

An orphan from the age of six, Mary McCarthy (1912–   ) was brought up between two sets of grandparents: the Catholic set and the Protestant/Jewish set. The period with the former was less happy than with the latter. In spite of the bitter accusation by her unbending maternal grandmother that her paternal grandfather was responsible for Mary's later agnosticism, it was he who was responsible for her attending a Sacred Heart convent school in Seattle where "the past still vibrated" with "the France of the Restoration."

Among her many books is the novel The Group, *a satirical analysis of the lives of eight graduates from Vassar, from which she too graduated. Its publication undoubtedly left the presidents of other women's colleges breathing a prayer of gratitude to that Supreme Being, about Whom Mary McCarthy harbors misgivings, that she had not graduated from their institutions however much lustre she would have added. The novel also occasioned a cartoon in* The New Yorker *of a bosomy prexy, be-capped and be-gowned, about to award a diploma to a bright-looking graduate but saying firmly words to this effect: "But first do you promise not to write a novel about your alma mater?"*

Memories of a Catholic Girlhood *is autobiographical and tells of simpler days.*

❋ I HAD achieved prominence not long before by publicly losing my faith and regaining it at the end of a retreat. I believe Elinor and Mary questioned me about this on the playground, during recess, and listened with serious, respectful faces while I told them about my conversations with the Jesuits. Those serious faces ought to have been an omen, but if the two girls used what I had revealed to make fun of me, it must have been behind my back. I never heard any more of it, and yet just at this time I began to feel something, like a cold breath on the nape of my neck, that made me wonder whether the new position I had won for myself in the convent was as secure as I imagined. I would turn around in study hall and find the two girls looking at me with speculation in their eyes.

It was just at this time, too, that I found myself in a perfectly absurd situation, a very private one, which made me live, from month to month, in horror of discovery. I had waked up one morning, in my convent room, to find a few small spots of blood on my sheet; I had somehow scratched a trifling cut on one of my legs and opened it during the night. I wondered what to do about this, for the nuns were fussy about bedmaking, as they were about our white collars and cuffs, and if we had an inspection those spots might count against me. It was best, I decided, to ask the nun on dormitory duty, tall, stout Mother Slattery, for a clean bottom sheet, even though she might scold me for having scratched my leg in my sleep and order me to cut my toenails. You never know what you might be blamed for. But Mother Slattery, when she bustled into look at the sheet, did not scold me at all; indeed, she hardly seemed to be listening as I explained to her about the cut. She told me to sit down: she would be back in a minute. "You can be excused from athletics today," she added, closing the door. As I waited, I considered this remark, which seemed to me strangely munificent, in view of the unimportance of the cut. In a moment, she returned, but without the sheet. Instead, she produced out of her big pocket a sort of cloth girdle and a peculiar flannel object which I first took to be a bandage, and I began to protest that I did not need or want a bandage; all I needed was a bottom sheet. "The sheet can wait," said Mother Slattery, succinctly, handing me two large safety pins. It was the pins that abruptly enlightened me; I saw Mother Slattery's mistake, even as she was instructing me as to how this flannel article, which I now understood to be a sanitary napkin, was to be put on.

"Oh, no, Mother," I said, feeling somewhat embarrassed. "You don't understand. It's just a little cut, on my leg." But Mother, again, was not listening; she appeared to have grown deaf, as the nuns had a habit of doing when what you were saying did not fit in with their ideas. And now that I knew what was in her mind, I was conscious of a funny constraint; I did not feel it proper to name a natural process, in so many words, to a nun. It was like trying not to think of their going to the bathroom or trying not to see the straggling iron-grey hair coming out of their coifs (the common notion that they shaved their heads was false). On the whole, it seemed better just to show her my cut. But when I offered to do so and unfastened my black stocking, she only glanced at my leg, cursorily. "That's only a scratch, dear," she said. "Now hurry up and put this on or you'll be late for chapel. Have you any pain?" "No, no, Mother!" I cried. "You don't understand!" "Yes, yes, I understand," she replied soothingly, "and you will too, a little later. Mother Superior will tell you about it some time during the morning. There's nothing to be afraid of. You have become a woman."

"I know all about that," I persisted. "Mother, please listen. I just cut my leg. On the athletic field. Yesterday afternoon." But the more excited I grew, the more soothing, and yet firm, Mother Slattery became. There seemed to be nothing for it but to give up and do as I was bid. I was in the grip of a higher authority, which almost had the power to persuade me that it was right and I was wrong. But of course I was not wrong; that would have been too good to be true. While Mother Slattery waited, just outside my door, I miserably donned the equipment she had given me, for there was no place to hide it, on account of drawer inspection. She led me down the hall to where there was a chute and explained how I was to dispose of the flannel thing, by dropping it down the chute into the laundry. (The convent arrangements were very old-fashioned, dating back, no doubt, to the days of Louis Philippe.)

The Mother Superior, Madame MacIllvra, was a sensible woman, and all through my early morning classes, I was on pins and needles, chafing for the promised interview with her which I trusted would clear things up. *"Ma Mère,"* I would begin, "Mother Slattery thinks . . ." Then I would tell her about the cut and the athletic field. But precisely the same impasse confronted me when I was summoned to her office at recess-time. I talked about my cut, and *she* talked about becoming a woman. It was rather like a round, in which she was singing "Scotland's burning, Scotland's burning," And I was singing "Pour on water, pour on water." Neither of us could hear the other, or, rather, I could hear her, but she could not hear me. Owing to our different positions in the convent, she was free to interrupt me, whereas I was expected to remain silent until she had finished speaking. When I kept breaking in, she hushed me, gently, and took me on her lap. Exactly like Mother Slattery, she attributed all my references to the cut to a blind fear of this new, unexpected reality that had supposedly entered my life. Many young girls, she reassured me, were frightened if they had not been prepared. "And you, Mary, have lost your dear mother, who could have made this easier for you." Rocked on Madame MacIllvra's lap, I felt paralysis overtake me and I lay, mutely listening, against her bosom, my face being tickled by her white, starched, fluted wimple, while she explained to me how babies were born, all of which I had heard before.

There was no use fighting the convent. I had to pretend to have become a woman, just as, not long before, I had had to pretend to get my faith back—for the sake of peace. This pretense was decidedly awkward. For fear of being found out by the lay sisters downstairs in the laundry (no doubt an imaginary contingency, but the convent was so very thorough), I reopend the cut on my leg, so as to draw a little blood to stain the napkins, which were issued me regularly, not only on this occasion, but every twenty-eight days thereafter. Eventually, I abandoned this bloodletting, for fear of lockjaw, and trusted to fate. Yet I was in awful dread of detection; my only hope, as I saw it, was either to be released from the convent or to become a woman in reality, which might take a year, at least, since I was only twelve. Getting out of athletics once a month was not sufficient compensation for the farce I was going through. It was not my fault; they had forced me into it; nevertheless, it was I who would look silly—worse than silly; half mad—if the truth ever came to light.

From *Memories of a Catholic Girlhood*
by Mary McCarthy

Helen Keller

Helen Keller (1880–1968) was born in Tuscumbia, Alabama, a normal baby. Nineteen months later she was deaf and blind, the result of an undiagnosed illness. Because she was deaf, she became mute. There was doubt about her mind. Her parents refused to believe it had been impaired, yet they could not reach her intelligence. To use her own later description, their daughter had become "a Phantom living in a world that was no-world."

For five years she lived in this no-world. She was rescued from it by Annie Sullivan, who at twenty-one came from Massachusetts to Alabama to serve as teacher to Helen Keller. "Teacher" she was called by her pupil (and others) for the rest of her life.

Visually handicapped herself, Annie Sullivan arrived at the Keller home on March 3, 1887, a date that Helen Keller treasured thereafter as her "soul's birthday." Teacher began at once spelling into Helen's hand, and like a quick, eager animal the child imitated her. The first weeks were strenuous. The dramatic fight between Annie Sullivan and the small Helen Keller in the play, and later the film, "The Miracle Worker," did indeed take place. It was one of several; in one battle Helen knocked out two of Ms. Sullivan's front teeth.

It took Annie Sullivan a month to reach Helen's human mind in the breakthrough described below. After that, progress was so rapid as to almost obscure the exhausting hours that made up the process. In a loving book about Annie Sullivan fittingly entitled Teacher, *Helen Keller described that early progression. After she had learned many nouns, there came adjectives. Finally Teacher introduced verbs. Gradually Helen began to ask basic questions previously beyond her conception—what, where, how, why. The answers from Teacher's hand ended the child's isolation. Teacher also taught her how to laugh and how to play.*

Which of these women was more remarkable? It would be impossible to say. Helen Keller received many honors in her lifetime; she always felt that the name of Annie Sullivan should be in tandem with hers. Annie Sullivan was until her death in 1936 Helen Keller's constant companion. A few weeks before she died someone, meaning to be kind, said to her, "Teacher you must get well. Without you Helen would be nothing." Annie Sullivan replied, "That would mean that I have failed."

Teacher and student both knew she had not failed.

❋ THE most important day I remember in all my life is the one on which my teacher, Anne Mansfield Sullivan, came to me. I am filled with wonder when I consider the immeasurable contrasts between the two lives which it connects. It was the third of March, 1887, three months before I was seven years old.

On the afternoon of that eventful day, I stood on the porch, dumb, expectant. I guessed vaguely from my mother's signs and from the hurrying to and fro in the house that something unusual was about to happen, so I went to the door and waited on the steps. The afternoon sun penetrated the mass of honeysuckle that covered the porch, and fell on my upturned face. My fingers lingered almost unconsciously on the familiar leaves and blossoms which had just come forth to greet the sweet southern spring. I did not know what the future held of marvel or surprise for me. Anger and bitterness had preyed upon me continually for weeks and a deep languor had succeeded this passionate struggle.

Have you ever been at sea in a dense fog, when it seemed as if a tangible white darkness shut you in, and the great ship, tense and anxious, groped her way toward the shore with plummet and sounding-line, and you waited with beating heart for something to happen? I was like that ship before my education began, only I was without compass or sounding-line, and had no way of knowing how near the harbour was. "Light! give me light!" was the wordless cry of my soul, and the light of love shone on me in that very hour.

I felt approaching footsteps. I stretched out my hand as I supposed to my mother. Some one took it, and I was caught up and held close in the arms of her who had come to reveal all things to me, and, more than all things else, to love me.

The morning after my teacher came she led me into her room and gave me a doll. The little blind children at the Perkins Institution had sent it and Laura Bridgman had dressed it; but I did not know this until afterward. When I had played with it a little while, Miss Sullivan slowly spelled into my hand the word "d-o-l-l." I was at once interested in this finger play and tried to imitate it. When I finally succeeded in making the letters correctly I was flushed with childish pleasure and pride. Running downstairs to my mother I held up my hand and made the letters for doll. I did not know that I was spelling a word or even that words existed; I was simply making my fingers go in monkey-like imitation. In the days that followed I learned to spell in this uncomprehending way a great many words, among them *pin, hat, cup* and a few verbs like *sit, stand* and *walk*. But my teacher had been with me several weeks before I understood that every thing has a name.

One day, while I was playing with my new doll, Miss Sullivan put my big rag doll into my lap also, spelled "d-o-l-l" and tried to make me understand that "d-o-l-l" applied to both. Earlier in the day we had had a tussle over the words "m-u-g" and "w-a-t-e-r." Miss Sullivan had tried to impress it upon me that "m-u-g" is *mug* and that "w-a-t-e-r" is *water,* but I persisted in confounding the two. In despair she had dropped the subject for the time, only to renew it at the first opportunity. I became impatient at her repeated attempts and, seizing the new doll. I dashed it upon the floor. I was keenly delighted when I felt the fragments of the broken doll at my feet. Neither sorrow nor regret followed my passionate outburst. I had not loved the doll. In the still, dark world in which I lived there was no strong sentiment or tenderness. I felt my teacher sweep the fragments to one side of the hearth, and I had a sense of satisfaction that the cause of my discomfort was removed. She brought me my hat, and I knew I was going out into the warm sunshine. This thought, if a wordless sensation may be called a thought, made me hop and skip with pleasure.

We walked down the path to the well-house, attracted by the fragrance of the honeysuckle with which it was covered. Someone was drawing water and my teacher placed my hand under the spout. As the cool stream gushed over one hand she spelled into the other the word *water*, first slowly, then rapidly. I stood still, my whole attention fixed upon the motions of her fingers. Suddenly I felt a misty consciousness as of something forgotten—a thrill of returning thought; and somehow the mystery of language was revealed to me. I knew then that "w-a-t-e-r" meant the wonderful cool something that was flowing over my hand. That living word awakened my soul, gave it light, hope, joy, set it free! There were barriers still, it is true, but barriers that could in time be swept away.

I left the well-house eager to learn. Everything had a name, and each name gave birth to a new thought. As we returned to the house every object which I touched seemed to quiver with life. That was because I saw everything with the strange, new sight that had come to me. On entering the door I remembered the doll I had broken. I felt my way to the hearth and picked up the pieces. I tried vainly to put them together. Then my eyes filled with tears; for I realized what I had done, and for the first time I felt repentance and sorrow.

I learned a great many new words that day. I do not remember what they all were; but I do know that *mother, father, sister, teacher* were among them—words that were to make the world blossom for me, "like Aaron's rod, with flowers." It would have been difficult to find a happier child than I was as I lay in my crib at the close of that eventful day and lived over the joys it had brought me, and for the first time longed for a new day to come.

From *The Story of My Life* by Helen Keller

Mrs. Ripley

Although Hamlin Garland (1860–1940) used the Midwest farm-lands where he grew up as setting for his fiction, "Mrs. Ripley's Trip" has a universal quality. His writings were regarded by some critics as "bitter pictures of the futility of farm lives."

Mrs. Ripley would not have looked upon her life as futile. Her life was purposeful, as indeed she herself was purposeful. She needed her trip, and she got it. After it was over, she was ready to go back to where she was needed, even if not visibly appreciated.

❋ THE night was in windy November, and the blast, threatening rain, roared around the poor little shanty of Uncle Ripley, set like a chicken-trap in the vast Iowa prairie. Uncle Ethan was mending his old violin, with many York State "dums!" and "I gol darns!" totally oblivious of his tireless old wife, who, having "finished the supper-dishes," sat knitting a stocking, evidently for the little grandson who lay before the stove like a cat.

Neither of the old people wore glasses, and their light was a tallow candle; they couldn't afford "none o' them new-fangled lamps." The room was small, the chairs were wooden, and the walls bare—a home where poverty was a never-absent guest. The old lady looked pathetically little, weazened, and hopeless in her ill-fitting garments (whose original color had long since vanished), intent as she was on the stocking in her knotted, stiffened fingers, and there was a peculiar sparkle in her little black eyes, and an unusual resolution in the straight line of her withered and shapeless lips.

Suddenly she paused, stuck a needle in the spare knob of her hair at the back of her head, and looking at Ripley, said decisively: "Ethan Ripley, you'll haff to do your own cooking from now on to New Year's. I'm goin' back to Yaark State."

The old man's leather-brown face stiffened into a look of quizzical surprise for a moment; then he cackled, incredulously: "Ho! Ho! har! Sho! be y', now? I want to know if y' be."

"Well, you'll fine out."

"Goin' to start to-morrow, mother?"

"No, sir, I ain't; but I am on Thursday. I want to get to Sally's by Sunday, sure, an' to Silas's on Thanksgivin'."

There was a note in the old woman's voice that brought genuine stupefaction into the face of Uncle Ripley. Of course in this case, as in all others, the money consideration was uppermost.

"Howgy 'xpect to get the money, mother? Anybody died an' left yeh a pile?"

"Never you mind where I get the money, so 's 't *you* don't haff to bear it. The land knows if I'd 'a' waited for *you* to pay my way—"

"You needn't twit me of bein' poor, old woman," said Ripley, flaming up after the manner of many old people. "I've done *my* part t' get along. I've worked day in and day out—"

"Oh! *I* ain't done no work, have I?" snapped she, laying down the stocking and levelling a needle at him, and putting a frightful emphasis on "I."

"I didn't say you hadn't done no work."

"Yes, you did!"

"I didn't neither. I said—"

"I *know* what you said."

"I said I'd done *my part!*" roared the husband, dominating her as usual by superior lung power. "I didn't *say* you hadn't done your part," he added with an unfortunate touch of emphasis.

"I know y' didn't *say* it, but y' meant it. I don't know what y' call doin' my part, Ethan Ripley; but if cookin' for a drove of harvest hands and thrashin' hands, takin' care o' the eggs and butter, 'n' diggin' 'taters an' milkin' ain't *my* part, I don't never expect to do my part, 'n' you might as well know it fust's last.

"I'm sixty years old," she went on, with a little break in her harsh voice, dominating him now by woman's logic, "an' I've never had a day to myself, not even Fourth o' July. If I've went a-visitin' 'r to a picnic, I've had to come home an' milk 'n' get supper for you menfolks. I ain't been away t' stay overnight for thirteen years in this house, 'n' it was just so in Davis County for ten more. For twenty-three years, Ethan Ripley, I've stuck right to the stove an' churn without a day or a night off."

Her voice choked again, but she rallied, and continued impressively, "And now I'm a-goin' back to Yaark State."

Ethan was vanquished. He stared at her in speechless surprise, his jaw hanging. It was incredible.

"For twenty-three years," she went on, musingly, "I've just about promised myself every year I'd go back an' see my folks." She was distinctly talking to herself now, and her voice had a touching, wistful cadence. "I've wanted to go back an' see the old folks, an' the hills where we played, an' eat apples off the old tree down by the well. I've had them trees an' hills in my mind days and days—nights, too—an' the girls I used to know, an' my own folks—"

She fell into a silent muse, which lasted so long that the ticking of the clock grew loud as a gong in the man's ears, and the wind outside seemed to sound drearier than usual. He returned to the money problem; kindly, though.

"But how y' goin' to raise the money? I ain't got no extra cash this time. Agin Roach is paid, an' the interest paid, we ain't go no hundred dollars to spare, Jane, not by a jugful."

"Wal, don't you lay awake nights studyin' on where I'm a-goin' to get the money," said the old woman, taking delight in mystifying him. She had him now, and he couldn't escape. He strove to show his indifference, however, by playing a tune or two on the violin.

"Come, Tukey, you better climb the wooden hill," Mrs. Ripley said, a half-hour later, to the little chap on the floor, who was beginning to get drowsy under the influence of his grandpa's fiddling. "Pa, you had orta 'a' put that string in the clock to-day—on the 'larm side the string is broke," she said, upon re-turning from the boy's bedroom. "I orta git up early to-morrow, to git some sewin' done. Land knows, I can't fix up much, but they is a little I c'n do. I want to look decent."

They were alone now, and they both sat expectantly.

"You 'pear to think mother, that I'm agin yer goin'."

"Wal, it would kinder seem as if y' hadn't hustled yerself any t' help me git off."

He was smarting under the sense of being wronged.

"Wal, I'm just as willin' you should go as I am for myself, but if I ain't got no money I don't see how I'm goin' to send—"

"I don't want ye to send; nobody ast ye to, Ethan Ripley. I guess if I had what I've earnt since we came on this farm I'd have enough to go to Jericho with."

"You've got as much out of it as I have," he replied gently. "You talk about you goin' back. Ain't I been wantin' to go back myself? And ain't I kep' still 'cause I see it wa'n't no use? I guess I've worked jest as long and as hard as you, an' in storms an' in mud an' heat, ef it comes t' that."

The woman was staggered, but she wouldn't give up; she must get in one more thrust.

"Wal, if you'd 'a' managed as well as I have, you'd have some money to go with." And she rose and went to mix her bread and set it "raisin'."

He sat by the fire twanging his fiddle softly. He was plainly thrown into gloomy retrospection, something quite unusual for him. But his fingers picking out the bars of a familiar tune set him to smiling, and whipping his bow across the strings, he forgot all about his wife's resolutions and his own hardships. "Trouble always slid off his back like punkins off a haystack, anyway," his wife said.

The old man still sat fiddling softly after his wife disappeared in the hot and stuffy little bedroom off the kitchen. His shaggy

head bent lower over his violin. He heard her shoes drop—*one,*
two. Pretty soon she called:

"Come, put up that squeakin' old fiddle, and go to bed. Seems
as if you orta have sense enough not to set there keepin' everybody in the house awake."

"You hush up," retorted he. "I'll come when I git ready, and
not till. I'll be glad when you're gone—"

"Yes, I warrant *that.*"

With which amiable good-night they went off to sleep, or at
least she did, while he lay awake pondering on "where under the
sun she was goin' t' raise that money."

The next day she was up bright and early, working away on
her own affairs, ignoring Ripley entirely, the fixed look of resolution still on her little old wrinkled face. She killed a hen and
dressed and baked it. She fried up a pan of doughnuts and made
a cake. She was engaged in the doughnuts when a neighbor came
in, one of these women who take it as a personal affront when
any one in the neighborhood does anything without asking their
advice. She was fat, and could talk a man blind in three minutes
by the watch. Her neighbor said:

"What's this I hear, Mis' Ripley?"

"I dun know. I expect you hear about all they is goin' on in
this neighborhood," replied Mrs. Ripley, with crushing blunt-
ness; but the gossip did not flinch.

"Well, Sett Turner told *me* that her husband told *her* that Ripley
told *him* this mornin' that you was goin' back East on a visit."

"Wal, what of it?"

"Well, air yeh?"

"The Lord willin' an' the weather permittin', I expect I be."

"Good land, I want to know! Well, well! I never was so astonished in my whole life. I said, says I, 'It can't be.' 'Well,'
ses 'e, 'tha's what *she* told me,' ses 'e. 'But,' says I, 'she is the
last woman in the world to go gallavantin' off East,' ses I. 'An','
ses he, 'but it comes from good authority,' ses he. 'Well, then,

it must be so,' ses I. But, land sakes! do tell me all about it. How come you to make up y'r mind? All these years you've been kind a' talkin' it over, an' now y'r actshelly goin'—well, I *never!* 'I s'pose Ripley furnishes the money,' ses I to him. 'Well, no,' ses 'e. 'Ripley says he'll be blowed if he sees where the money's coming from,' ses 'e; and ses I 'But maybe she's jest jokin',' ses I. 'Not much,' he says. S' 'e: "Ripley believes she's goin' fast enough. He's jest as anxious to find out as we be—' "

Here Mrs. Doudney paused for breath; she had walked so fast and rested so little that her interminable flow of "ses I's" and "ses he's" ceased necessarily. She had reached, moreover, the point of most vital interest—the money.

"An' you'll find out jest 'bout as soon as he does," was the dry response from the figure hovering over the stove; and with all her manoeuvring that was all she got.

All day Ripley went about his work exceedingly thoughtful for him. It was cold blustering weather. The wind rustled among the corn-stalks with a wild and mournful sound, the geese and ducks went sprawling down the wind, and the horses' coats were ruffled and backs raised.

The old man was husking all alone in the field, his spare form rigged out in two or three ragged coats, his hands inserted in a pair of gloves minus nearly all the fingers, his thumbs done up in "stalls," and his feet thrust into huge coarse boots. The "down ears" wet and chapped his hands, already worn to the quick. Toward night it grew colder and threatened snow. In spite of all these attacks he kept his cheerfulness, and though he was very tired, he was softened in temper.

Having plenty of time to think matters over, he had come to the conclusion that the old woman needed a play-spell. "I ain't likely to be no richer next year than I am this one; if I wait till I'm able to send her she won't never go. I calc'late I c'n git enough out o' them shoats to send her. I'd kind a' lotted on eat'n' them pigs done up in sassengers, but if the ol' woman goes East,

Tukey an' me'll kind a' haff to pull through without 'em. We'll have a turkey f'r Thanksgivin', an' a chicken once 'n a while. Lord! but we'll miss the gravy on the flapjacks." (He smacked his lips over the thought of the lost dainty.) "But let 'er rip! We can stand it. Then there is my buffalo overcoat. I'd kind a' calc'lated on havin' a buffalo—but that's gone up the spout along with them sassengers."

These heroic sacrifices having been determined upon, he put them into effect at once.

This he was able to do, for his corn-rows ran alongside the road leading to Cedarville, and his neighbors were passing almost all hours of the day.

It would have softened Jane Ripley's heart could she have seen his bent and stiffened form among the corn-rows, the cold wind piercing to the bone through his threadbare and insufficient clothing. The rising wind sent the snow rattling among the moaning stalks at intervals. The cold made his poor dim eyes water, and he had to stop now and then to swing his arms about his chest to warm them. His voice was hoarse with shouting at the shivering team.

That night as Mrs. Ripley was clearing the dishes away she got to thinking about the departure of the next day, and she began to soften. She gave way to a few tears when little Tewksbury Gilchrist, her grandson, came up and stood beside her.

"Gran'ma, you ain't goin' to stay away always, are yeh?"

"Why, course not, Tukey. What made y' think that?"

"Well, y' ain't told us nawthin' 't all about it. An' yeh kind o' look 's if yeh was mad."

"Well, I ain't mad; I'm jest a-thinkin', Tukey. Y' see, I come away from them hills when I was a little girl a'most; before I married y'r grandad. And I ain't never been back. 'Most all my folks is there, soony, an' we've been s' poor all these years I couldn't seem t' never git started. Now, when I'm 'most ready t' go, I feel kind a queer—'s if I'd cry."

And cry she did, while little Tewksbury stood patting her trembling hands. Hearing Ripley's step on the porch, she rose hastily and, drying her eyes, plunged at the work again.

Ripley came in with a big armful of wood, which he rolled into the wood-box with a thundering crash. Then he pulled off his mittens, slapped them together to knock off the ice and snow, and laid them side by side under the stove. He then removed cap, coat, blouse, and finally his boots, which he laid upon the wood-box, the soles turned toward the stove-pipe.

As he sat down without speaking, he opened the front doors of the stove, and held the palms of his stiffened hands to the blaze. The light brought out a thoughtful look on his large, uncouth, yet kindly, visage. Life had laid hard lines on his brown skin, but it had not entirely soured a naturally kind and simple nature. It had made him penurious and dull and iron-muscled; had stifled all the slender flowers of his nature; yet there was warm soil somewhere hid in his heart.

"It's snowin' like all p'ssessed," he remarked finally. "I guess we'll have a sleigh-ride to-morrow. I calc'late t' drive y' daown in scrumptious style. If you must leave, why, we'll give yeh a whoopin' old send-off—won't we, Tukey?"

Nobody replying, he waited a moment. "I've ben a-thinkin' things over kind o' t'-day, mother, an' I've come t' the conclusion that we *have* been kind o' hard on yeh, without knowin' it, y' see. Y' see I'm kind o' easy-goin', an' little Tuke he's only a child, an' we ain't c'nsidered how you felt."

She didn't appear to be listening, but she was, and he didn't appear, on his part, to be talking to her, and he kept his voice as hard and dry as he could.

"An' I was tellin' Tukey t'-day that it was a dum shame our crops hadn't turned out better. An' when I saw ol' Hatfield go by I hailed him, an' asked him what he'd gimme for two o' m' shoats. Wal, the upshot is, I sent t' town for some things I calc'late you'd need. An' here's a ticket to Georgetown, and ten dollars. Why, ma, what's up?"

Mrs. Ripley broke down, and with her hands all wet with dishwater, as they were, covered her face, and sobbed. She felt like kissing him, but she didn't. Tewksbury began to whimper too; but the old man was astonished. His wife had not wept for years (before him). He rose and walking clumsily up to her and timidly touched her hair—

"Why, mother! What's the matter? What've I done now? I was calc'latin' to sell them pigs anyway. Hatfield jest advanced the money on 'em."

She hopped up and dashed into the bedroom, and in a few minutes returned with a yarn mitten, tied around the wrist, which she laid on the table with a thump, saying: "I don't want yer money. There's money enough to take me where I want to go."

"Whew—ew! Thunder and gimpsum root! Where 'd ye get that? Didn't dig it out of a hole?"

"No, I jest saved it—a dime at a time—see!"

Here she turned it out on the table—some bills, but mostly silver dimes and quarters.

"Thunder and scissors! Must be two er three hundred dollars there," he exclaimed.

"They's jest seventy-five dollars and thirty cents; just about enough to go back on. Tickets is fifty-five dollars, goin' and comin'. That leaves twenty dollars for other expenses, not countin' what I've already spent, which is six-fifty," said she, recovering her self-possession. "It's plenty."

"But y'ain't calc'lated on no sleepers nor hotel bills."

"I ain't goin' on no sleeper. Mis' Doudney says it's jest scandalous the way things is managed on them cars. I'm goin' on the old-fashioned cars, where they ain't no half-dressed men runnin' around."

"But *you* needn't be afraid of them, mother; at your age—"

"There! you needn't throw my age an' homeliness into my face, Ethan Ripley. If I hadn't waited an' tended on you so long, I'd look a little more's I did when I married yeh."

Ripley gave it up in despair. He didn't realize fully enough how the proposed trip had unsettled his wife's nerves. She didn't realize it herself.

"As for the hotel bills, they won't be none. I ain't agoin' to pay them pirates as much for a day's board as we'd charge for a week's, and have nawthin' to eat but dishes. I'm goin' to take a chicken an' some hard-boiled eggs, an' I'm goin' right through to Georgetown."

"Wal, all right, mother; but here's the ticket I got."

"I don't want yer ticket."

"But you've got to take it."

"Well, I haint."

"Why, yes, ye have. It's bought, an' they won't take it back."

"Won't they?" She was perplexed again.

"Not much they won't I ast 'em. A ticket sold is sold."

"Wal, if they won't—"

"You bet they won't."

"I s'pose I'll haff to use it." And that ended it.

They were a familiar sight as they rode down the road toward town next day. As usual, Mrs. Ripley sat up straight and stiff as "a half-drove wedge in a white-oak log." The day was cold and raw. There was some snow on the ground, but not enough to warrant the use of sleighs. It was "neither sleddin' nor wheelin'." The old people sat on a board laid across the box, and had an old quilt or two drawn up over their knees. Tewksbury lay in the back part of the box (which was filled with hay), where he jounced up and down, in company with a queer old trunk and a brand-new imitation-leather hand-bag.

There is no ride quite so desolate and uncomfortable as a ride in a lumber-wagon on a cold day in autumn, when the ground is frozen, and the wind is strong and raw with threatening snow.

The wagon-wheels grind along in the snow, the cold gets in under the seat at the calves of one's legs, and the ceaseless bumping of the bottom of the box on the feet is almost intolerable.

There was not much talk on the way down, and what little there was related mainly to certain domestic regulations, to be strictly followed, regarding churning, pickles. pancakes, etc. Mrs. Ripley wore a shawl over her head, and carried her queer little black bonnet in her hand. Tewksbury was also wrapped in a shawl. The boy's teeth were pounding together like castanets by the time they reached Cedarville, and every muscle ached with the fatigue of shaking.

After a few purchases they drove down to the station, a frightful little den (common in the West), which was always too hot or too cold. It happened to be hot just now—a fact which rejoiced little Tewksbury.

"Now git my trunk *stamped,* 'r *fixed,* 'r whatever they call it," she said to Ripley, in a commanding tone, which gave great delight to the inevitable crowd of loafers beginning to assemble. "Now remember, Tukey, have grandad kill that biggest turkey night before Thanksgiving, an' then you run right over to Mis' Doudney's—she's got a nawful tongue, but she can bake a turkey first-rate—an' she'll fix up some squash-pies for yeh. You can warm up one o' them mince-pies. I wish ye could be with me, but ye can't; so do the best ye can."

Ripley returning now, she said: "Wal, now, I've fixed things up the best I could. I've baked bread enough to last a week, an' Mis' Doudney has promised to bake for yeh—"

"I don't like her bakin'."

"Wal, you'll haff to stand it till I get back, 'n' you'll find a jar o' sweet pickles an' some crab-apple sauce down suller, 'n' you'd better melt up brown sugar for 'lasses, 'n' for goodness' sake don't eat all of them mince-pies up the fust week, 'n' see that Tukey ain't froze goin' to school. An' now you'd better get out for home. Good-by! an' remember them pies."

As they were riding home, Ripley roused up after a long silence.

"Did she—a—kiss you good-by, Tukey?"

"No, sir," piped Tewksbury.

"Thunder! didn't she?" After a silence: "She didn't me, neither. I guess she kind a' sort a' forgot it, bein' so flustered, y' know."

One cold, windy, intensely bright day, Mrs. Stacey, who lives about two miles from Cedarville, looking out of the window, saw a queer little figure struggling along the road, which was blocked here and there with drifts. It was an old woman laden with a good half-dozen parcels, which the wind seemed determined to wrench from her.

She was dressed in black, with a full skirt, and her cloak being short, the wind had excellent opportunity to inflate her garments and sail her off occasionally into the deep snow outside the track, but she held out bravely till she reached the gate. As she turned in, Mrs. Stacey cried:

"Why! it's Gran'ma Ripley, just getting back from her trip. Why! how do you do? Come in. Why! you must be nearly frozen. Let me take off your hat and veil."

"No, thank ye kindly, but I can't stop," was the given reply. "I must be gittin' back to Ripley. I expec' that man has jest let ev'rything go six ways f'r Sunday."

"Oh!, you *must* sit down just a minute and warm."

"Wal, I will; but I've got to git home by sundown sure. I don't s'pose they's a thing in the house to eat," she said solemnly.

"Oh, dear! I wish Stacey was here, so he could take you home. An' the boys at school—"

"Don't need any help, if 't wa'nt for these bundles an' things. I guess I'll jest leave some of 'em here, an'— Here! take one of these apples. I brought 'em from Lizy Jane's suller, back to Yaark State."

"Oh! they're delicious! You must have had a lovely time."

"Pretty good. But I kep' thinkin' of Ripley an' Tukey all the time. I s'pose they have had a gay time of it" (she meant the opposite of gay). "Wal, as I told Lizy Jane, I've had my spree, an' now I've got to git back to work. They ain't no rest for such as we are. As I told Lizy Jane, them folks in the big houses have Thanksgivin' dinners every day of their lives, and men an' women in splendid clo's to wait on 'em, so 't Thanksgivin' don't mean anything to 'em; but we poor critters, we make a great to-do if we have a good dinner onct a year. I've saw a pile o' this world, Mrs. Stacey—a pile of it! I didn't think they was so many big houses in the world as I saw b'tween here an' Chicago. Wal, I can't set here gabbin'." She rose resolutely. "I must get home to Ripley. Jest kind o' stow them bags away. I'll take two an' leave them three others. Good-by! I must be gittin' home to Ripley. He'll want his supper on time."

And off up the road the indomitable little figure trudged, head held down to the cutting blast—little snow-fly, a speck on a measureless expanse, crawling along with painful breathing, and slipping, sliding steps—"Gittin' home to Ripley an' the boy."

Ripley was out to the barn when she entered, but Tewksbury was building a fire in the old cook-stove. He sprang up with a cry of joy, and ran to her. She seized him and kissed him and it did her so much good she hugged him close, and kissed him again and again, crying hysterically.

"Oh, gran'ma, I'm so glad to see you! We've had an awful time since you've been gone."

She released him, and looked around. A lot of dirty dishes were on the table, the table-cloth was a "sight to behold" (as she afterward said), and so was the stove—kettle-marks all over the table-cloth, splotches of pancake batter all over the stove.

"Wal, I sh'd say as much," she dryly assented, untying her bonnet-strings.

When Ripley came in she had her regimentals on, the stove

was brushed, the room swept, and she was elbow-deep in the dish-pan. "Hullo, mother! Got back, hev yuh?"

"I sh'd say it was about *time*," she replied curtly, without looking up or ceasing work. "Has ol' 'Crumpy' dried up yit?" This was her greeting.

Her trip was a fact now; no chance could rob her of it. She had looked forward twenty-three years toward it, and now she could look back at it accomplished. She took up her burden again, never more thinking to lay it down.

From "Mrs. Ripley's Trip," *Main-Travelled Roads* by Hamlin Garland

Marie Curie

Marie Sklodowska Curie (1867–1934), chemist and physicist, and her husband, Pierre, discovered both polonium and radium, in 1898. For their work on radioactivity they shared, with Becquerel, the 1903 Nobel Prize in Physics.

The first time Pierre, an esteemed scientist, asked Marie, then a student already showing genius, to marry him she refused; to live in France away from her family and Poland seemed unthinkable. She went home for the summer, and his letters followed her. In October she returned to Paris to complete her work at the Sorbonne. When it was finished she planned, in spite of Pierre's entreaties, to return to Poland. At the end of ten months, however, she wrote to a girlhood friend, "I am about to marry the man I told you about last year in Warsaw. It is a sorrow for me to have to stay forever in Paris, but what am I to do? Fate has made us deeply attached to each other, and we cannot endure the idea of separating."

The Curies had been married less than eleven years when Pierre was killed by a team of horses pulling a heavy wagon. Madame Curie's daughter, Eve, wrote that from the moment the three words "Pierre is dead" reached her mother's consciousness "a cope of solitude and secrecy fell upon her shoulders forever." She became "not only a widow but at the same time a pitiful and incurably lonely woman."

Excerpts from her diary in the early months following Pierre's death bear witness to this:

                                                April, 1906

PIERRE, my Pierre, you are there, calm as a poor wounded man resting in sleep, with his head bandaged. Your face is sweet and serene, it is still you, lost in a dream from which you cannot get out. Your lips, which I used to call greedy, are livid and colorless. Your little beard is gray. Your hair can hardly be seen, because the wound begins there, and above the forehead, on the right, the bone that broke can be seen. Oh! how you have suffered, how you have bled, your clothes are soaked in blood, What a terrible shock your poor head has felt, you poor head that I so often caressed in my two hands. I kissed your eyelids which you used to close so that I could kiss them, offering me your head with a familiar movement. . . .

We put you into the coffin Saturday morning, and I held your head up for this move. We kissed your cold face for the last time. Then a few periwinkles from the garden on the coffin and the little picture of me that you called "the good little student" and that you loved. It is the picture that must go with you into the grave, the picture of her who had the happiness of pleasing you enough so that you did not hesitate to offer to share your life with her, even when you had seen her only a few times. You often told me that this was the only occasion in your life when you acted without hesitation, with the absolute conviction that you were doing well. My Pierre, I think you were not wrong. We were made to live together, and our union had to be.

Your coffin was closed and I could see you no more. I didn't allow them to cover it with the horrible black cloth. I covered it with flowers and I sat beside it.

. . . They came to get you, a sad company; I looked at them, and did not speak to them. We took you back to Sceaux, and we saw you go down into the big deep hole. Then the dreadful procession of people. They wanted to take us away. Jacques and I resisted. We wanted to see everything to the end. They filled the grave and put sheaves of flowers on it. Everything is over, Pierre is sleeping his last sleep beneath the earth; it is the end of everything, everything, everything. . . .

May, 1906

I am offered the post of successor to you, my Pierre: your course and the direction of your laboratory. I have accepted. I don't know whether this is good or bad. You often told me you would have liked me to give a course at the Sorbonne. And I would like at least to make an effort to continue your work. Sometimes it seems to me that this is how it will be most easy for me to live, and at other times it seems to me that I am mad to attempt it.

May 7, 1906

My Pierre, I think of you without end, my head is bursting with it and my reason is troubled. I do not understand that I am to live henceforth without seeing you, without smiling at the sweet companion of my life.

For two days the trees have been in leaf and the garden is beautiful. This morning I looked at the children there. I thought you would have found them beautiful and that you would have called me to show me the periwinkles and the narcissus in bloom. Yesterday, at the cemetery, I did not succeed in understanding the words "Pierre Curie" engraved on the stone. The beauty of the countryside hurt me, and I put my veil down so as to see everything through my crepe.

May 11, 1906

My Pierre, I got up after having slept rather well, relatively calm. That was only a quarter of an hour ago, and now I want to howl again—like a wild beast.

May 14, 1906

My little Pierre, I want to tell you that the laburnum is in flower, the wistaria, the hawthorn and the iris are beginning—you would have loved all that.

I want to tell you, too, that I have been named to your chair, and that there have been some imbeciles to congratulate me on it.

I want to tell you that I no longer love the sun or the flowers. The sight of them makes me suffer. I feel better on dark days like the day of your death, and if I have not learned to hate fine weather it is because my children have need of it.

May 22, 1906

I am working in the laboratory all day long, it is all I can do: I am better off there than anywhere else. I conceive of nothing any more that could give me personal joy, except perhaps scientific work—and even there, no, because if I succeeded with it, I could not endure you not to know it.

June 10, 1906

Everything is gloomy. The preoccupations of life do not even allow me time to think of my Pierre in peace.

From *Madame Curie* by Eve Curie

Mama

"Is good." *These are the warming words with which Kathryn Forbes' Mama expresses approval, pleasure, satisfaction. The first story about Mama—the one that follows—appeared in the* Reader's Digest *in the early forties. People wanted more. Soon there was a collection of stories about her in a volume entitled* Mama's Bank Account, *then a play,* I Remember Mama. *At the end of the seventies the play became a musical with Liv Ullmann playing Mama and music by Richard Rodgers.*

Mama is the heart of a loving, closely-knit Norwegian family in San Francisco. The family also includes Papa, Nels, Katrin, Christine, Dagmar (and her cherished tom-cat, Uncle Elizabeth), and the baby, Kaaren. One watches the family become "Americanized" at the same time that it struggles to keep its old-world values.

Her dream is that someday there will be enough bourders so all the leaves will have to be put in the dining room table.

One of their boarders, an aviator, took people for rides over the Marina every Sunday. He invited a longing, eager Papa to join him. Mama at first disapproved, so Papa would not go. Then secretly she ventured to fly. Afterwards she said to Papa, "You are right. It is wonderful. . . . I go up today to see if it is safe. Is all right now for you to go."

As Mama says, "Life is good. Life is so good."

❋ For as long as I could remember, the small cottage on Castro Street had been home. The familiar background was there; Mama, Papa, my only brother, Nels. There was my sister Christine, closest to me in age, yet ever secret and withdrawn—and the littlest sister, Dagmar.

There, too, came the Aunts, Mama's four sisters. Aunt Jenny, who was the oldest and the bossiest; Aunt Sigrid; Aunt Marta; and our maiden Aunt, Trina.

The Aunts' old bachelor uncle, my Great-uncle Chris—the "black Norwegian"—came with his great impatience, his shouting and stamping. And brought mystery and excitement to our humdrum days.

But the first awareness was of Mama.

I remember that every Saturday night Mama would sit down by the scrubbed kitchen table and with much wrinkling of usually placid brows count out the money Papa had brought home in the little envelope.

There would be various stacks.

"For the landlord," Mama would say, piling up the big silver pieces.

"For the grocer." Another group of coins.

"For Katrin's shoes to be half-soled." And Mama would count out the little silver.

"Teacher says this week I'll need a notebook." That would be Christine or Nels or I.

Mama would solemnly detach a nickel or a dime and set it aside.

We would watch the diminishing pile with breathless interest.

At last, Papa would ask, "Is all?"

And when Mama nodded, we could relax a little and reach for schoolbooks and homework. For Mama would look up then and smile. "Is good," she'd murmur. "We do not have to go to the Bank."

It was a wonderful thing, that Bank Account of Mama's. We were all so proud of it. It gave us such a warm, secure feeling. No one else we knew had money in a big bank downtown.

I remember when the Jensens down the street were put out because they couldn't pay their rent. We children watched the big strange men carry out the furniture, took furtive notice of poor

Mrs. Jensen's shamed tears, and I was choked with sudden fear. This, then, happened to people who did not have the stack of coins marked "Landlord." Might this, could this, violence happen to us?

I clutched Christine's hands. *"We* have a Bank Account," she reassured me calmly, and suddenly I could breathe again.

When Nels graduated from grammar school he wanted to go on to High. "Is good," Mama said, and Papa nodded approvingly.

"It will cost a little money," Nels said.

Eagerly we brought up chairs and gathered around the table. I took down the gaily painted box that Aunt Sigrid had sent us from Norway one Christmas and laid it carefully in front of Mama.

This was the "Little Bank." Not to be confused, you understand, with the big Bank downtown. The "Little Bank" was used for sudden emergencies, such as the time Christine broke her arm and had to be taken to a doctor, or when Dagmar got croup and Papa had to go to the drugstore for medicine to put into the steam kettle.

Nels had it all written out neatly. So much for carfare, for clothes, for notebooks and supplies. Mama looked at the figures for a long time. Then she counted out the money in the Little Bank. There was not enough.

She pursed her lips. "We do not," she reminded us gently, "want to have to go to the Bank."

We all shook our heads.

"I will work in Dillon's grocery after school," Nels volunteered.

Mama gave him a bright smile and laboriously wrote down a sum and added and subtracted. Papa did it in his head. He was very quick on arithmetic. "Is not enough," he said. Then he took his pipe out of his mouth and looked at it for a long time. "I give up tobacco," he said suddenly.

Mama reached across the table and touched Papa's sleeve, but she didn't say anything. Just wrote down another figure.

"I will mind the Elvington children every Friday night," I said. "Christine can help me."

"Is good," Mama said.

We all felt very good. We had passed another milestone without having to go downtown and draw money out of Mama's Bank Account. The Little Bank was sufficient for the present.

So many things, I remember, came out of the Little Bank that year. Christine's costume for the school play, Dagmar's tonsil operation, my Girl Scout uniform. And always, in the background, was the comforting knowledge that should our efforts fail, we still had the Bank to depend upon.

Even when the Strike came, Mama would not let us worry unduly. We all worked together so that the momentous trip downtown could be postponed. It was almost like a game.

During that time Mama "helped out" at Kruper's bakery for a big sack of only slightly stale bread and coffeecake. And as Mama said, fresh bread was not too good for a person and if you put the coffeecake into the hot oven it was nearly as nice as when first baked.

Papa washed bottles at the Castro Creamery every night and they gave him three quarts of fresh milk and all the sour milk he could carry away. Mama made fine cheese.

The day the Strike was over and Papa went back to work, I saw Mama stand a little straighter, as if to get a kink out of her back.

She looked around at us proudly. "Is *good*," she smiled. "See? We did not have to go down to the Bank."

That was twenty years ago.

Last year I sold my first story. When the check came I hurried over to Mama's and put the long green slip of paper in her lap. "For you," I said, "to put in your Bank Account."

And I noticed for the first time how old Mama and Papa looked. Papa seemed shorter, now, and Mama's wheaten braids were sheened with silver.

Mama fingered the check and looked at Papa.

"Is good," she said, and her eyes were proud.

"Tomorrow," I told her, "you must take it down to the Bank."

"You will go with me, Katrin?"

"That won't be necessary, Mama. See? I've endorsed the check to you. Just hand it to the teller, he'll deposit it to your account."

Mama looked at me. "Is no account," she said. "In all my life, I never been inside a Bank."

And when I didn't—couldn't—answer, Mama said earnestly: "Is not *good* for little ones to be afraid—to not feel secure."

From *Mama's Bank Account* by Kathryn Forbes

Caroline Norton

Caroline Sheridan Norton (1808–1877) was the granddaughter of Richard Brinsley Sheridan. A writer herself, she became more widely known for her eventful life than for her writings. Responsible for this was her husband, George Norton, who sued for divorce and named Lord Melbourne as co-respondent.

The Age and The Satirist, two tabloids of their day, sensationalized the case in every way and attacked by innuendos not only Mrs. Norton but also her brothers and sisters and friends. Norton lost the suit but he was given custody of the children and was allowed to collect his wife's literary earnings. In addition, fifteen years later when his mother-in-law died, he inherited the life-interest of his wife's inheritance from her father.

In England at the time of Norton's suit—the mid 1830s—divorce was under the jurisdiction of the ecclesiastical courts which had to follow canon law. These courts could grant a divorce from bed and board, that is, a decree of judicial separation leaving the couple married while forbidding cohabitation, but could not grant a total divorce from the marriage bond. This power lay only in Parliament. In 1857, by act of Parliament, judicial courts succeeded to the jurisdiction over nullity and partial dissolution and were given the added power to grant total dissolution.

Jane Gray Perkins, an early biographer of Mrs. Norton, does not attempt to credit her with securing passage of the Marriage Act of 1857. She does feel, however, that it was Caroline Norton's influence respecting lesser reforms that make the Act, to some extent, a Bill of Rights for married women. Unquestionably two of her works, English Law for Women in the Nineteenth Century *(1854) and* A Letter to the Queen *(1855) both helped to bring about improvement in the status of married women.*

✳ MR. NORTON having thus failed in his suit for damages, was no longer in a position to continue his action to divorce his wife, and she was equally unable to divorce him because, on returning to him in 1835, a few months before their last quarrel, she had condoned all her husband's worst acts of cruelty and infidelity against her, and was no longer able to bring them up as evidence in her case before the courts.

There was nothing left for them, therefore, but to find some terms for a legal separation. Such separations differed practically very little from a divorce granted by Doctors' Commons, as the ecclesiastical divorce court was sometimes called. . . .

George Norton was a lawyer, and he knew exactly how much and how little the law required of him. His first statement of what he proposed to do in this matter he sent to his wife's brother almost immediately after his wife's departure from his house, and its terms were almost an insult, for he proposed to give her nothing at all—except immunity from his society. As for the rest, her family might support her, or she might earn her living by writing, while he kept the children entirely in his own hands, her access to them being dependent on his good pleasure. After the trial he was constrained to offer an allowance of 300 pounds a year, still keeping in his hands the possession of all his children.

She wrote entreating that she might be permitted to see them. The youngest was already in town, having been brought up by his nurse when she was called to testify at the trial. This child the mother was permitted to see at her brother's house for half an hour in the presence of his nurse and another of the women witnesses. . . .

But her request to see the other children was granted only on condition she came to the chambers of Mr. Norton's attorney, where they might be brought for half an hour by two of the women witnesses at the trial, who were ordered to remain in the room during the interview. To this proposition was appended a note by his own solicitor:

"Mr. Norton has made the appointment to see the children here. I cannot but regret it."

This offer she refused in a letter to her own legal adviser to be transmitted to her husband.

"However bitter it may be to me, I must decline seeing my children in the manner proposed. I say nothing of the harshness— the inhumanity of telling me I must either see them at the chambers of his solicitor or not at all; but I say it is not decent that the father of those children should force me, their mother, out of the very tenderness I bear them, to visit them at the chambers of the attorney who collected the evidence, examined the witnesses, and conducted the proceedings for the intended divorce. I say it is not decent—nay that even if I were guilty, it would not be decent to make me such a proposition. But I am innocent. I have been pronounced and publicly declared innocent by the noble-man against whom that ill-advised action was brought. . . ."

Eventually the children were allowed to come to her brother's house in Grosvenor Square—only for half an hour. . . .

She met them once by stealth, as they were taking their morn-ing walk in St. James Park. She tells of this encounter some-where.

"My eldest, who is seven years old, gave me a little crumpled letter which he said he had had in his pocket a fortnight directed to me, but that none of the servants would put it in the post. He was so dear and intelligent, and listened so attentively to all I said to him that it was a great, though melancholy satisfaction to have had this interview. I know he will never forget me. . . ."

For four years their mother not only never saw them, but seldom even knew where they were. . . .

But from such mischievous tyranny on the part of her husband there was no appeal, because there was no law; there was hardly any public opinion to interfere with a father's absolute right over his children to the exclusion of their mother, if he chose so to assert it.

That, in the end, after four years of unremitted struggle on her part, she did regain some limited intercourse with her three little boys while they were still children, was because she, single-handed, was able to effect a change in a law so that it would never again be possible for a man like George Norton to vent his spite in this particular way on the woman who was unfortunate enough to be his wife and to have incurred his resentment. . . .

On the whole, however, she submitted to the obvious necessity of a woman to bear, in matters like this, the greater share of blame. She submitted to Lord Melbourne's request that she would make no public attempt to clear her name of the scandals which still besmirched it. On one point alone she refused to remain passive. She knew it was the law of England which had taken her children away from her. Very well, then; that law must be changed, or if that was beyond her power, at least known through the length and breadth of the land in its whole iniquity.

Mrs. Norton was back in England again early in 1840, busy as usual with law and lawyers. This time, however, thanks to her own exertions, she had some part of the law on her side.

The new Act permitted any mother who was denied access to her young children, if she could prove by affidavit that her own character was above reproach, to petition the Lord Chancellor for a hearing before a special court, composed of the Lord Chancellor, the Master of the Rolls, or other Chancery judges. The court, if convinced of the justice of her cause, could grant her access to her children when and how it thought best. . . .

And, after all, the case never came to a public hearing; but this only because George Norton at the last minute withdrew his opposition and proposed to compromise.

"He yielded," his wife says bitterly, "simply so far as the law would have compelled him, and as was necessary to save himself from the threatened and certain exposure which my appeal under the new laws would have entailed. I saw my children in the most formal and comfortless manner. . . ."

But her children were never really given back to her on the terms she demanded, "to be with her at all times, that she might direct their education," until a tragic accident had deprived her forever of the youngest of them, and the very pain of a common bereavement had compelled a gentler spirit in her husband.

In the autumn of 1842 all three children were, as usual, with their father on his Yorkshire estate of Kettlethorpe, when Willie, the baby, by that time grown to be a little lad of eight years old, out riding alone on his pony, was thrown and, though he was only slightly hurt by the fall, blood-poisoning set in from neglect of a bad scratch he had received on his arm and he died before the arrival of his mother who had been sent for when his condition was judged more serious. In her words: "Sir Fitzroy and Lady Kelly (who was a stranger to me) met me at the railway station. I said: 'I am here. Is my boy better?'

" 'No', she said, 'he is not better, he is dead.' And I found, instead of a child, a corpse already coffined. . . ."

There was still a struggle with her husband before he would bind himself by legal agreement to admit her to a fair share of the companionship of the two children left to her. There is a letter on this subject written to her sisiter.

Dearest Georgie,

I am so nervous that I can't even express myself, having my own affairs just talked over and hanging on a hair. Talfourd is most kind and earnest. They have yielded the point about the children. I am to be with them half the year, but Norton wants to force me to live at Kettlethorpe that half-year, which would never do. That is, in fact, his having them all the year and letting me see them five months. I am, in fear and trembling, standing firm for their actual residence under my own roof. Pray answer me by return of post if only a single line, whether you and Co. think me right. I am so afraid of missing them altogether, and yet so afraid that if I give in I shall be cheated.

"Ever yours
"Carrie

The question of residence was finally decided in her favour . . .

Caroline Norton was not thirty-seven when she went to live alone in Chesterfield Street. Beautiful, impulsive, and unconventional, it was impossible she should not have drawn down upon herself some portion of that blame which is so easily expended upon a woman separated from her husband, who still desires to please, and has a natural liking for men's society. Some of the gossip talked about her was, no doubt, quite groundless; though for some it is possible that she herself gave occasion if not actual material.

It would have been strange indeed if she had not sometimes grown restive under the endless prohibitions of her lot, that woman's divorce of which she was one day to speak so bitterly:

"Alone, married to a man's name, but never to know the protection of this nominal husband, nor the joys of family, nor the every-day companionship of a real home. Never to feel or show preference for any friend not of her own sex, though tempted, perhaps, by a feeling nobler than passion—gratitude for generous pity, that has lightened the dreary days. To be slandered, tormented, insulted; to find the world and the world's law utterly indifferent to her wrongs or her husband's sin; and through all this to lead a chaste, unspotted, patient, cheerful life; without anger, without bitterness, and with meek respect for those edicts which, with a perverse parody on Scripture, pronounce that it 'is not good for man to be alone, but extremely good for woman. . . .' "

From *The Life of Mrs. Norton* by Jane Gray Perkins

Jane Eyre

I cannot tell whether I find Jane Eyre *(published first in 1847) remarkable for itself only, or also because of Charlotte Brontë, its author. I know that I find it one of the tenderest of love stories and Jane a woman of intelligence and passion, a new type of heroine for the mid-nineteenth century. She was not, according to her own description, a beautiful woman—". . . I sometimes regretted that I was not handsomer: I sometimes wished to have rosy cheeks, a straight nose, and small cherry mouth. . . ."*

She was the creation of Charlotte Brontë, herself a woman of intelligence and passion, whose own life was one of sacrifice and social isolation. She did not marry until her fortieth year, and a year later died of pregnancy toxemia. Jane Eyre *resulted largely from her lively imagination rather than her experiences, although these too were present to a degree.*

Jane Eyre *was an orphan and her story is told autobiographically. Brought up in a charity school after having been rejected by an aunt by marriage, Jane, barely eighteen, accepts a position as governess at Thornfield to Adele, the ward of Edward Rochester. Rochester, master of Thornfield, falls deeply in love with Jane and she with him. The marriage date is set only to be spoiled by news that Rochester is already married to a woman hopelessly insane and for whose care he provides at Thornfield. Jane leaves, eventually finding another position, and she lives with the Reverend St. John River (who wishes to marry her, not because he loves her, but because she would be a help to him in his future missionary work in India) and his sisters, Mary and Diana.*

One night she senses Rochester needs her. She returns to Thornfield where she finds the mansion gutted as a result of a fire set by Rochester's lunatic wife who then killed herself. Rochester in an effort to save her and the servants is blinded and his right hand injured so as to necessitate amputation. Jane finds him in this maimed condition, but also finds happiness for both of them.

❄ READER, I married him. A quiet wedding we had: he and I, the parson and clerk, were alone present. When we got back from church, I went into the kitchen of the manor-house, where Mary was cooking the dinner, and John cleaning the knives, and I said:

"Mary, I have been married to Mr. Rochester this morning." The housekeeper and her husband were both of the decent phlegmatic order of people, to whom one may at any time safely communicate a remarkable piece of news without incurring the danger of having one's ears pierced by some shrill ejaculation, and subsequently stunned by a torrent of wordy wonderment. Mary did look up, and she did stare at me: the ladle with which she was basting a pair of chickens roasting on the fire, did for some three minutes hang suspended in the air; and for the same space of time John's knives also had a rest from the polishing process; but Mary, bending again over the roast, said only—

"Have you, Miss? Well, for sure!"

A short time after she pursued: "I seed you go out with the master, but I didn't know you were gone to church to be wed"; and she basted away. John when I turned to him was grinning from ear to ear.

"I told Mary how it would be," he said: "I knew what Mr. Edward" (John was an old servant, and had known his master when he was the cadet of the house, therefore, he often gave him his Christian name)—"I knew what Mr. Edward would do; and I was certain he would not wait long neither; and he'd done right, for aught I know. I wish you joy, Miss!" and he politely pulled his forelock.

"Thank you, John. Mr. Rochester told me to give you and Mary this." I put into his hand a five-pound note. Without waiting to hear more, I left the kitchen. In passing the door of that sanctum some time after, I caught the words, "She'll happen do better for him nor ony o' t' grand ladies." And again, "If she ben't one o' the' handsomest, she's noan faal and varry good-natured; and i' his een she's fair beautiful, onybody may see that."

I wrote to Moor House and to Cambridge immediately to say what I had done: fully explaining also why I had thus acted. Diana and Mary approved the step unreservedly. Diana announced that she would just give me time to get over the honeymoon, and then she would come and see me.

"She had better not wait till then, Jane," said Mr. Rochester, when I read her letter to him; "if she does, she will be too late, for our honey-moon will shine our life-long; its beams will only fade over your grave or mine."

My tale grows to its close: one word respecting my experience of married life, and one brief glance at the fortunes of those whose names have most frequently recurred in this narrative, and I have done.

I have now been married for ten years. I know what it is to live entirely for and with what I love best on earth. I hold myself supremely blest—blest beyond what language can express; because I am my husband's life as fully as he is mine. No woman was ever nearer to her mate than I am: ever more absolutely bone of his bone, and flesh of his flesh. I know no weariness of my Edward's society: he knows none of mine, any more than we each do of the pulsation of the heart that beats in our separate bosoms; consequently, we are ever together. To be together is for us to be at once as free as in solitude, as gay as in company. We talk, I believe, all day long: to talk to each other is but a more animated and an audible thinking. All my confidence is bestowed on him, all his confidence is devoted to me; we are precisely suited in character—perfect concord is the result.

Mr. Rochester continued blind the first two years of our union: perhaps it was that circumstance that drew us so very near—that knit us so very close! for I was then his vision, as I am still his right hand. Literally, I was (what he often called me) the apple of his eye. He saw nature—he saw books through me; and never did I weary of gazing for his behalf, and of putting into words the effect of field, tree, town, river, cloud, sunbeam—of the landscape before us; of the weather round us—and impressing by sound of his ear what light could no longer stamp on his eye. Never did I weary of reading to him; never did I weary of conducting him where he wished to go: of doing for him what he wished to be done. And there was a pleasure in my services, most full, most exquisite, even though sad—because he claimed these services without painful shame or damping humiliation. He loved me so truly, that he knew no reluctance in profiting by my attendance: he felt that I loved him so fondly, that to yield that attendance was to indulge my sweetest wishes.

One morning at the end of the two years, as I was writing a letter to his dictation, he came and bent over me, and said:

"Jane, have you a glittering ornament round your neck?"

I had a gold watch-chain: I answered "Yes."

"And have you a pale blue dress on?"

I had. He informed me then, that for some time he had fancied the obscurity clouding one eye was becoming less dense; and that now he was sure of it.

He and I went up to London. He had the advice of an eminent oculist; and he eventually recovered the sight of that one eye. He cannot now see very distinctly: he cannot read or write much; but he can find his way without being led by the hand: the sky is no longer a blank to him—the earth no longer a void. When his first-born was put into his arms, he could see that the boy had inherited his own eyes, as they once were—large, brilliant, and black. On that occasion, he again, with a full heart, acknowledged that God had tempered judgment with mercy.

My Edward and I, then, are happy and the more so, because those we most love are happy likewise.

From *Jane Eyre* by Charlotte Brontë

Angie

Maureen Daly (1921–   ) was a senior at Rosary College, River Forest, Illinois, when her novel, Seventeenth Summer, *was published. It is the story of Angie Morrow's summer, a summer about which she was to exclaim at its end "and yet never again would there ever be anything quite as wonderful as that seventeenth summer." Within the year, the book had gone into nine printings. Her classmates took a vicarious pride in its success, and her next door neighbor in the college residence hall claimed she should have a share in its royalties since its typing late into the night had cost her many hours of sleep.*

The novel, written by an author whose own seventeenth summer was only shortly behind her, has other autobiographical touches. Although Maureen Daly was born in Ireland, the family moved to Fond du Lac, Wisconsin, the setting she provided for Angie and her family. The Daly family consisted of four girls just as did the Morrow family. Ms. Daly's chronological place in the family corresponded with Angie's. The portrayal of Angie's mother was very much like Mrs. Daly—inner strength, standards high, firm. Angie said of her family, "We aren't the kind of family who love each other out loud." The same might have been said of the Dalys.

Seventeenth Summer is the story of first love. It begins with a first date and first kiss, and unfolds through the summer. In July comes Jack's first declaration of love when he says, "I've thought about this for a long time and I know what I'm saying . . . I'm in love with you, Angie!" And a few short weeks later he bursts out, "Angie, I never knew being in love took so much time."

Fall comes early that year. Early and suddenly. Angie, incredulous, questions her mother, "How could it happen, Mom? How could it end over night?" Her mother answers, "It's always been like that, Angie. You just haven't been old enough to notice before."

✳ ON Friday night before the dance I stood in the garden, wondering what it was all about. Just a short time ago Jack called to say he would pick me up at a quarter-past nine. I was all ready except to slip my evening dress on over my head. In the end we had decided on the sprigged dimity and my mother had pressed it so the full skirt hung in soft, billowy folds and the small sleeves stuck up stiff and puffed as it was spread out on my bed. I had come out to the garden to pick bachelor's-buttons for my hair in my long white slip, holding it high to keep the hem above the cool dew on the grass. And as I stood in the garden with the soft air against my cheek and a night breeze fingering through my hair, I couldn't help wondering a little. . . .

I know you will think it's terrible, after I had only been out with him three times but in a way I couldn't help it—even if I did know from the very beginning of the evening, or at least from the first dance, that it would happen. If I had heard of any other girl's doing it I would probably think the same thing you will think but, well, I did it—and I wish I could make you understand.

I can't explain much about it—the dance itself, I mean. So much happened that I don't remember any of it very distinctly; but it doesn't matter much, because it wasn't the dance, it was the evening as a whole that was so important. . . .

I don't know just the minute it began to happen but soon, after each dance, when the music had stopped, I would feel less and less like taking my arm away from Jack's shoulder and he kept holding my hand as if the music were still playing. And yet he would never look at me and as I watched his face it was perfectly still, as if nothing were happening, while all the time his hand was in mine sending warm shivers all up my arm. Once Swede danced past and said under his breath, "Break it up, break it up!" and Jack grinned suddenly and I couldn't help laughing.

The band was playing something slow and hushed—I don't

remember what it was—but it filled the room from the floor to the ceiling. No one seemed to be actually dancing but the crowd moved with a slow, rhythmic swaying and Jack and I seemed to be part of the whole gentle movement. I shut my eyes and the sound of the other dancers, the full, sweet swelling of the saxophone, and the thin magic of the clarinet floated above us in a haunted cloud while we danced in a breathless stillness beneath. I knew then I couldn't go on feeling this way—I knew something had to happen.

The rest of the evening passed quickly, like a movie film being run off in a rapid blur, rushing to the climax. When the dance was almost over we went out on the terrace, Jack and I. I think there were several other people out there, I'm not sure, though I vaguely remember the scattered glow of cigarettes burning in the half darkness and the warm sound of people laughing. It seemed to me then that I had two hearts, one where it should be and the other pulsing rapidly in the soft hollow at the base of my throat. Leaning against the clubhouse wall I could feel the roughness of the stone and the coolness of the Virginia creeper leaves on my shoulders. Even out here the air throbbed with music. It was better to say something casual than just to wait in that breathless silence saying nothing at all. "Did you have a good time in Green Bay, Jack?" I asked.

"I did, Angie. I really had fun," he answered. "I meant to send you a postcard but, well, I just didn't get around to it." He paused. Now it was his turn to be without words. "Did you do anything special while I was away? Anything interesting?" It was silly to be standing there with my hands closed tight behind my back telling him about the new book I had read and that Kitty had started to take swimming lessons at the lake to try to earn a Junior Lifesaver's badge and other unimportant things, when we both knew we were just trying to make conversation, just marking time; and the words lumped in my throat, not even wanting to be said. It was silly just standing there. Both of us knew.

"I used to caddy on this course," he told me suddenly as if

the thought were an inspiration. "It's a beautiful course. Beautiful, Angie. One of the best in the state. I practically know it by heart. There's a little elevation over by the second hole, you can't see it from here, but standing on it you can look out over the whole course. At night it's wonderful. There's just enough moon—would you like to look at it with me?" I nodded and he took my hand to guide me over the grass. "Hold your skirt up," he said softly. "There is dew on everything."

Standing on that elevation, the whole course seemed to be rolled out broad before us in the moonlight, smoothness and shadow. From this distance a sand trap looked like a big open scar on the smooth face of the green and the moon gave a weird yellow half-light that made the whole night a two-tone picture of highlights and hollows. Behind us tall old elm trees on the edge of the course stretched their black leaf-lace high against the sky. Jack took a handkerchief out of his coat and the dubonnet dress handkerchief from his breast pocket, spreading them on the grass for me to sit on. I have never known anything so lovely as that night.

At first neither of us spoke but sat feeling the softness of the breeze and watching the fireflies winking in the grass, while from the clubhouse music floated out to us, muted by the almost tangible stillness of the night. Jack lit a cigarette and in the match glow I saw his face, so young and clean, and the sheer joy of just being with him made me shiver a little. He smoked in silence for a time and then, turning to me, said unexpectedly, almost as if he relished the words, "Everyone I introduced you to tonight liked you, Angie. A couple of the fellows are mad that they didn't find you first." I didn't say anything but sat looking at the moon—by squinting my eyes I could make it shoot out into long yellow jags of light. . . .

All around us the crickets were keeping up a steady cheep-cheep, so constant that after a while it was no sound at all, just a rhythm keeping time to the faster beating of my heart. Then without looking at me, without turning his head, Jack asked, "Why, Angie?" The night was so quiet that the words seemed to stand still in mid-air, echoing over and over softly till at last they faded away. Why? I could hear my thoughts brushing past each other in my head, none of them coherent enough to be spoken. There were no words for an answer. I felt Jack's hand on mine as it lay on the grass, his fingers warm and hesitant. He flipped his cigarette away and together we watched the stub glowing until it burned itself out in the grass.

Really I don't know how it happened. If I could tell you I would. Maybe I shouldn't even mention it, seeing it was only the third time I had been out with him. But I knew it was going to happen, and I wanted it to.

It was wonderfully strange knowing even before he moved, even before he put his arm around me, that he would. It gave me a new sense of power to think that from the very beginning of the evening—at least, from the first dance— I knew this would happen.

Then suddenly, and yet it wasn't sudden at all, I remember myself with both hands pressed against the gabardine of his coat so hard that I could feel the roughness of the cloth. My head seemed to be throbbing wildly and still I was thinking very clearly and precisely. Behind him I could see the high stars and the golf course stretched out silver-green in the moonlight and the fireflies flickering in the grass like bits of neon lighting. I felt a new, breathless caution as if I were sitting in a bubble. And then I, Angie Morrow, who had never done anything like this before, who until last Monday night had never even had a real date, could feel his cheek on mine, as warm and soft as peach fuzz. And I knew if I moved my face just a little, just a very little. . . .

In the movies they always shut their eyes but I didn't. I didn't think of anything like that, though I do remember a quick thought passing through my mind again about how much he smelled like

Ivory soap when his face was so close to mine. In the loveliness of the next moment I think I grew up. I remember that behind him was the thin, yellow arc of moon, turned over on its back, and I remember feeling my hands slowly relax on the rough lapels of his coat. Sitting on the cool grass in my new sprigged dimity with the little blue and white bachelor's buttons pinned in my hair, Jack kissed me and his lips were as smooth and baby-soft as a new raspberry.

The night was so still I hardly noticed the small breeze that brushed past us, as soft and silent as a pussy willow.

From *Seventeenth Summer* by Maureen Daly

Louisa May Alcott

On the day of her birth, the father of Louisa May Alcott *(1832–1888) wrote that she was "a very fine healthful child—and has a fine foundation for health and energy of character." She did, indeed, show energy of character throughout her life. This was hardly surprising when one considers the strength of character of her mother, the idealism of her father, the atmosphere of the home in which she was brought up, the distinguished persons who were family friends, none being of greater help than Ralph Waldo Emerson.*

Her life embodied both adventure and quiet. On the adventuresome side one might cite the hiding of a runaway slave by her family when she was still a child, her nursing in Washington during the Civil War (an experience from which she never physically completely recovered), her literary successes, her acclaim in this country and abroad.

The quiet side of her life is reflected in her novel Little Women *which is autobiographical (and one of the most popular books ever written for girls). The four girls of the Alcott family are the four girls of the March family. Louisa is Jo March both in character and in her place as the second oldest daughter. Mrs. Alcott is Marmee. Neither the Alcotts nor the Marches were free from financial worries.*

It was often asked whether Louisa Alcott sold her beautiful hair as represented in Little Women. *She never did, but she regarded it as a possible resource in case of need. In her journal she wrote, "I will pay my debts, if I have to sell my hair to do it." She inquired of a barber how much it would be worth. She paid every debt her impractical father had incurred.*

The death in the novel of Beth is actually her sister's death about which Louisa May Alcott writes poignantly in her journal.

✳ FEBRUARY—A mild month; Betty very comfortable, and we hope a little.

Dear Betty is slipping away, and every hour is too precious to waste, so I'll keep my lamentations over Nan's (affairs) till this duty is over.

Lizzie makes little things, and drops them out of windows to the school-children, smiling to see their surprise. In the night she tells me to be Mrs. Gamp, when I give her lunch, and tries to be gay that I may keep up. Dear little saint! I shall be better all my life for these sad hours with you.

March 14th—My dear Beth died at three this morning, after two years of patient pain. Last week she put her work away, saying the needle was "too heavy," and having given us her few possessions, made ready for the parting in her own simple, quiet way. For two days she suffered much, begging for ether, though its effect was gone. Tuesday she lay in Father's arms, and called us round her, smiling contentedly as she said, "All here!" I think she bid us good by then, as she held our hands and kissed us tenderly. Saturday she slept, and at midnight became unconscious, quietly breathing her life away till three; then, with one last look of the beautiful eyes, she was gone.

، A curious thing happened, and I will tell it here, for Dr. G. said it was a fact. A few moments after the last breath came, as Mother and I sat silently watching the shadow fall on the dear little face, I saw a light mist rise from the body, and float up and vanish in the air. Mother's eyes followed mine, and when I said, "What did you see?" she described the same light mist. Dr. G. said it was the life departing visibly.

For the last time we dressed her in her usual cap and gown, and laid her on her bed—at rest at last. What she had suffered was seen in the face; for at twenty-three she looked like a woman of forty, so worn was she, and all her pretty hair gone.

On Monday Dr. Huntington read the Chapel service, and we

sang her favorite hymn. Mr. Emerson, Henry Thoreau, Sanborn, and John Pratt, carried her out of the old home to the new one at Sleepy Hollow chosen by herself. So the first break comes, and I know what death means—a liberator for her, a teacher for us.

My twenty-sixth birthday on the 29th. Some sweet letters from home, and a ring of A.'s and J.'s hair as a peace-offering. A quiet day, with many thoughts and memories.

The past year has brought us the first death and betrothal—two events that change my life. I can see that these experiences have taken a deep hold, and changed or developed me. Lizzie helps me spiritually, and a little success makes me more self-reliant. Now that Mother is too tired to be wearied with my moods, I have to manage them alone, and am learning that work of head and hand is my salvation when disappointment or weariness burden and darken my soul.

In my sorrow I think I instinctively came nearer to God, and found comfort in the knowledge that he was sure to help when nothing else could.

A great grief has taught me more than any minister, and when feeling alone I find refuge in the Almighty Friend. If this is experiencing religion I have done it; but I think it is only the lesson one must learn as it comes, and I am glad to know it.

After my fit of despair I seem to be braver and more cheerful, and grub away with a good heart. Hope it will last, for I need all the courage and comfort I can get.

I feel as if I could write better now—more truly of things I have felt and therefore *know*. I hope I shall yet do my great book, for that seems to be my work, and I am growing up to it. I even think of trying the "Atlantic." There's ambition for you! I'm sure some of the stories are very flat. If Mr. L. takes the one Father carried to him, I shall think I can do something.

From *Louisa May Alcott—Her Life, Letters, and Journals,* edited by Ednah B. Cheney

Krystyna Zywulska

Pawiak Prison in Warsaw is today a museum displaying artifacts from its horror years as a prison under German occupation in the Second World War. On the lighter side, the same playing cards handled by the fortune-teller mentioned below are there in an exhibit case—begrimed and oft-used, hand-made by prisoners.

I have known well only one person who was interned in a concentration camp (an extraordinary woman still living in Warsaw, and well-known as a journalist and radio commentator). It was she who gave me the book (I Came Back by Krystyna Zywulska) from which this selection was taken. Inside its cover she wrote, ". . . everything that she tells is TRUE and has to warn humanity," signing the inscription not only with her name but with her prisoner's number, 49439—a number still visible on her arm.

My friend too was a prisoner in Pawiak—one day she toured the prison-museum with me. She too had made packs of playing cards for the prisoners to use to while away their time. She too had been moved from Pawiak to a German camp, not to Auschwitz but to Ravensbrück. She too had been on a train that moved off to song—song that came after a cheer from one of the male prisoners as the women were loaded on to the cattle car: "We salute our beautiful, our strong, our courageous Polish women."

And she too came back.

✻ THE fortune-teller flipped her greasy cards and looked up at me, gloating over the effect of her prophecy.

"Yes, officials, a journey, a cross."

The cards had foretold the same future for each one of us in cell 44 of the Pawiak prison. We stared at them forebodingly, thinking of just one thing, the transport to Oswiecim. We had become accustomed to the Pawiak. Here there were fleas, beatings, even executions; we were afraid of them but we were horribly afraid of the transport.

At times when it was quiet at the Pawiak, one could hear the distant sounds of wheels, the clang of the street-car, echoes of the city. At the Pawiak one received messages from home and, although we who were arrested by the Gestapo never really believed that we would be released, we were aware that freedom was only one step away. But if they should take us to Oswiecim—we could not picture it. Not one of us knew what it really was, and not one of us wanted to know. Of one thing we were certain—from Oswiecim no one ever returned.

The grating of the turning key shattered the silence. An SS man, Wykup, one of the terrors of Pawiak, was standing in the doorway, his face like a death skull. Our apprehension and the fortune-teller's words were already coming true. Names were read, mine was the third on the list. Stiff-legged I walked out of the cell, followed by the sighs of those who remained. Zosha, white-lipped, stood at my side. I tried to smile.

"Well, we won't die yet."

"We won't die but we'll suffer and that's worse."

"Did you think you'd go free? After all, people do live there, and anyway, it's good we're going together. Cheer up. The others are looking at us. Don't look sad."

"You're right. I was only . . . At first . . . because my family wrote that they were trying . . ."

"Did you think it would work?"

"I sort of thought it would."

"Well, let's think that we'll come back. It depends a little on us."

"I think a lot depends on us."

She said this mechanically.

"Smile!"

Zosha smiled, and when her face lit up she charmed me as she had that first day—was it a year ago—when I offered her identification papers which both she and I knew were false and she had accepted without a word. Zosha was the superintendent of an apartment house. I needed the apartment. This slim, dark young woman with the delicate face not only protected me from the police but joined me in work for the underground. The Gestapo had arrested us at the same time and we had been lucky enough to stay together. Now her smile, a warm good-humoured smile that never could show a belief in bad fortune, said to me, "You'll see. It won't be so terrible."

At that moment Wykup passed. He looked as if he would strike her but he too seemed a little surprised by her bright face. He dropped his arm and walked on.

They crowded us into the transport cell. There we met women from other cells and floors; women who came from the solitary and the quarantine, women who had been at Pawiak for a whole year and who thought they had been forgotten, and those who had arrived a month ago and still bore signs of the free out-of-doors, traces of the sun which never showed itself in the Pawiak cells.

In the transport cell, some of the women began to pray, others tried to recall everything they knew about Oswiecim and about concentration camps in general. Others still, found release in banter.

"They'll give you a beautiful hair-do." (We knew our heads would be shaved.)

"They'll give you a number so you won't get lost."

"You'll live in virtue. You can't even talk to men . . ."

"Shut up," Stefa snapped. Her black eyes flamed beneath smooth hair that, combed madonna-wise, gave a deceptively placid aspect to her nervous, sensitive face. She bit her lips to keep back the tears—she was always on the verge of tears. She pressed my hand and began to talk about the young son she had left at home; she could not believe that she might never see him again. His eyes haunted her. She felt that he was blaming her because she had allowed them to take her away—because she, his wise mother, had been helpless against this worthless trash.

"What is he doing now?" she kept repeating tearfully. "My little one, he's waiting for me. Oh God, when they find out that I've been transported . . ."

I could not listen to her. A lump was rising in my throat.

"Stefa, we really shouldn't cry—we're not the first."

Nothing helped. I looked around the cell. The jokes and the lively talk died down. More and more of us began to cry until one deep spasm shook us all. It seemed that this sob would burst the prison wall and give us back our freedom and—Warsaw. But the walls did not burst—no miracle happened. Mrs. Pawlicz from cell 43 had an attack of hysteria. She jumped to the middle of the cell and began to flail her arms and legs. Her lips twisted in a frightful grin.

"Do you know where we're going? We're going to a party. You never saw such a party. I'm wearing my new hat. Look at all the pretty young women who are coming to the party. You'll dance to their music. You'll see."

She frothed at the mouth and her eyes turned up. We placed her on a bunk. She called out wildly at intervals and then grew silent.

"Well, girls, let's pray and then get some sleep," somebody said.

We knelt down. A chorus of an evening prayer reached us from another cell. A damp August evening looked in through the small grating above. Somewhere, so near and yet so far, people were walking along the Vistula, Stefa's little son was sleeping, my mother was keeping a wakeful watch.

Not many of us slept that night.

At six in the morning, Wykup came in and told us to get out just as we stood.

We were counted and our names were read from the transport list. Everything was in order. We were led out immediately after.

The Pawiak dogs barked angrily. Not one of us had taken either bread or clothing. Wykup had told us we would return. He said they would only count us. Everything we had accumulated—the food given us by those who stayed behind—everything was left in the transport cell.

Frightened, sleepy and tired we walked to the Pawiak courtyard. Pale-faced men looked through the windows; about eight hundred of them were going in the same transport, the largest ever to leave the prison.

One of the SS men, counting, pushing, shouting, arranged us in columns of five. Finally the trucks arrived and we were taken to the station.

We raced through the city under the escort of helmeted guards armed with machine guns. People on their way to work glanced fearfully at the crowded trucks and tried to recognize friends. I looked for someone I knew, perhaps someone who would hail me, but never saw a familiar face. They loaded us into cattle cars and secured all the openings.

"We're buried alive," someone groaned.

They shunted us from one track to another, to and fro, backwards and forwards until finally the wheels began to spin and the train moved forward. I don't know how it happened, but all at once from all corners of the car our voices rose in a spontaneous song—"Land of Our Fathers, We'll not abandon Thee."

The train moved faster and drowned the melody and the words. It tapped out the dreadful truth that lay at the end of our journey: to Oswiecim—to Oswiecim. At ten in the evening we stopped in an open field.

"*Aussteigen!*" Our car was opened. There were dogs again, a large number of them, barking, howling and straining towards us.

And again in columns of five the SS drove us on. We walked in silence.

The camp lay ahead of us. We moved closer and closer. The

electric-charged wire fence gleamed through the darkness, and the sentry-boxes made tall silhouettes against the sky. Each measured step echoed in our brains.

"So that's it—that's how it looks!" I thought, glancing at Zosha.

She knew I was looking at her, but was afraid to return my glance. Her head was held high, her lips were tightly closed. Just then we entered the camp. I turned around and calmly told myself, "I'm in the camp. This is Oswiecim—*Vernichtungslager*—there is no return from here."

"We've entered Hell." Zosha spoke in a quiet, distant voice. Then she added bitterly—"Do you think we'll roast?"

"I think we'll die in some other way. I don't know how. Don't look up. Don't look at the wire fence. Look at the barracks— look how many there are. People like us are sleeping in them. There will be work in the morning. Remember, the war will end pretty soon . . . we'll try to survive Zosha," I urged, "we must promise each other that we won't let anything break us . . . only death—perhaps!"

We were pushed into a hut and we lay down on the floor. One thought kept revolving in our heads so that we could not sleep nor lie quietly because of it.

What would tomorrow bring?

From *I Came Back* by Krystyna Zywulska

Amelia Earhart

Amelia Earhart (1898–1937), born in Atchinson, Kansas, had a knack of uttering casually momentous statements. This was befitting a pioneer pilot, as was her appearance: slim, carefree hair, infectious smile, intelligent expression.

Once she earned her pilot's license (lessons paid for with the money she earned working in a telephone office) her next ambition was to own a plane. By her twenty-fifth birthday she was the owner of a small biplane. Her first career, however, was that of social work.

It was G. P. Putnam of the well-known publishing firm who helped to catapult her to fame. Because of his wide range of acquaintances he had been asked to find a woman pilot to fly the Atlantic on a good will flight between England and America. He was introduced to Amelia Earhart. Soon the headlines of Boston papers proclaimed BOSTON SOCIAL WORKER TO FLY ATLANTIC and GIRL PILOT DARES THE ATLANTIC. She made the flight (not solo) in 1928.

In 1931 Amelia Earhart and G. P. Putnam were married. He declared he had proposed to her six times, the last being in the Lockheed hangar while she was waiting for her plane to warm up. She simply nodded her head, then patted his arm and climbed quickly aboard.

Her final adventure was an around-the-world flight with a co-pilot in 1937 but her plane was lost, under mysterious circumstances, somewhere between New Guinea and Howland Island in the Pacific.

But perhaps her most famous flight was a solo crossing of the Atlantic in 1932 which is described in a biography (Courage is the Price) *written by her sister, Muriel. The title is taken from a poem which Amelia wrote as a young woman:*

Courage is the price which life exacts for granting peace.
The soul that knows it not, knows no release
From little things . . .

✳ KNOWING Amelia's desire to advance aviation, GP was not surprised when she remarked one morning, over the breakfast buttermilk, "Would you mind if I flew across the Atlantic alone this spring?" Within a matter of minutes, GP had arranged a meeting with Bernt Balchen, a skilled Norwegian flier, who, they decided, was the man to master-mind this flight.

After explaining her projected undertaking, Amelia asked him soberly, "Bernt, do you think I am ready for this flight? Will you help me?"

Bernt, a man of few words, said only, "Yes, you can do it, Amelia, and yes, I will help."

It was early April when Amelia made her decision to attempt a solo crossing of the Atlantic. The following eight weeks were filled with rigorous conditioning of Amelia and her Lockheed Vega. Eddie Gorski, an expert Lockheed mechanic, was recruited by Bernt. In order to avoid the publicity which would hamper her training regimen, she chartered her plane to Bernt who was known to be considering an antarctic flight. Amelia had flown the red and gold Vega for nearly three years, so there was nothing unusual in having all ailerons replaced and a new engine and auxiliary fuel tanks installed, presumably for Mr. Balchen's Polar journey. Several new instruments now decorated the instrument panel: a drift indicator, two compasses, and a directional gyrocompass. For this flight, as Amelia had declared four years before, there were to be no pontoons.

"I'll just have to keep going until I get to land," she said, half jokingly, to GP. "You know I hate to get my hair wet!"

By the time the lovely pink and white dogwoods on the grounds of the Putnam home in Rye had dropped their blossoms, Amelia and the plane were poised for flight. As in the *Friendship* adventure, Dr. Kimball of the United States Weather Bureau furnished invaluable data and personally checked and rechecked conditions along the coast toward Newfoundland and as far out over the Atlantic as possible. There is little doubt that Dr. Kimball knew the reason for GP's haunting his office and for Amelia's more-than-passing interest in the Atlantic ceiling, but he never hinted at their secret.

On the morning of May nineteenth, GP telephoned Amelia at the Teterboro Airport where the Lockheed was garaged. Amelia was preparing for another short flight to practice instrument flying because the early forecasts had been unfavorable. She was called to the telephone in the hangar. Eddie had just spun the propeller, and Bernt was in the cockpit, when Amelia frantically waved to them to come to her at the telephone booth.

As the two men came near her, she called excitedly, "Bernt, GP says Doc gives us good visibility to Newfoundland and pretty far out. Let's go, shall we?"

Bernt wasted no words. "Okay," he said. "Okay with you, Eddie?"

Eddie nodded. "Sure, she's been ready to go for more than a week. Today suits me fine."

Amelia spoke to GP again. "The boys are ready and I'll get my things from Rye so we can leave early this afternoon. Cheerio!"

Amelia drove as rapidly as she dared back to Rye. She slipped into tan jodhpurs, white silk shirt, and a mannish windbreaker whose plainness she relieved by tying a gay blue and brown scarf around her neck. She tucked a toothbrush and a comb in a case and put it in her pocket. Stopping in the kitchen, she told the housekeeper not to prepare dinner for them that evening. Her flying suit was already folded under the co-pilot's seat in the Vega and she knew two cans of juice were in the map rack. There was nothing else she planned to carry on her trip to Europe. At the airport, GP gave her a folded twenty-dollar bill with the husbandly advice to telephone him as soon as she landed.

Bernt and Eddie were to fly Amelia to Harbor Grace so she could start the long night's flight refreshed. Amelia slept on the floor of the fuselage with her suit as a pillow as the plane winged its way north. In three hours Bernt set the plane down at Saint John, New Brunswick. The next morning they flew into Harbor Grace, the take-off point. While the men refueled the auxiliary tanks, Amelia picked up the telegrams that had arrived during the night. One from Dr. Kimball confirmed his earlier fair skies report, but warned of foul weather south of the regular Atlantic crossing lanes. GP's telegram was characteristically unsentimental: "Have booked passage on ship tomorrow night. Will join you in France." Amelia stopped at a small restaurant near the airfield and had her thermos bottle filled with hot tomato soup; then she started toward her plane which was warming up on the runway.

A fringe of sycamore trees cast long shadows in the early evening. The fragrance of spring was in the air. Life must have seemed very sweet as Amelia looked from the greening fields to the rocky shores and the restless waves beyond. Had anyone asked her what force impelled her to risk her life alone over the seemingly limitless expanse of water, I imagine she would have said with a shrug and a smile, "Why, for the fun of it, of course!"

In her heart she would have admitted that the real reason for this flight was to wipe out the stigma she felt at being only a passenger on the *Friendship*. Amelia, however, was thoroughly convinced that safe flying was important for the United States and the world; hence, each flight had to open an exciting frontier which eventually would become commonplace. "In just four years," she mused, "see how much planes have improved. Who knows where we will be flying next?"

Bernt's voice broke into Amelia's reverie, "Come, come now, Meely, you must be on your way to catch the tide!"

Smiling at his pretended gruffness, Amelia fastened her helmet and climbed into the pilot's seat. Carefully she made the routine checks, and finally tested the ailerons. Then, leaning out of the cockpit window, she shouted above the motors' roar, "Thank you both, again, and goodbye!"

"Skoal, Amalie!" called Bernt, using the Norwegian version of her name, as he held both arms aloft in a victory salute.

Amelia was airborne soon after seven o'clock on the evening of May twentieth. Within an hour, she was engaged in a duel for life between the elements and the Vega. Ice formed on the wings as she sought altitude to avoid the swirling fog which was covering the water. She set a course due east, flying as near the surface of the water as she dared to keep the wings free from the treacherous slush. At about eleven o'clock, the plane was hit by a heavy squall, and as Amelia glanced at the altimeter, she was appalled to see the dials spinning around and around. Somehow during the buffeting of the storm, the delicate adjustment of the instrument had been disturbed, so now Amelia was like a ship without a sounding lead sailing among hidden reefs. The clouds that had obscured the moon were suddenly blown away and Amelia saw the heaving seas not more than seventy-five feet below—a pretty narrow margin of safety. Amelia blessed Bernt for insisting that she have a gyrocompass installed in the plane, for now she saw that her speed indicator was as inaccurate as her altimeter, and that she must navigate solely by the tiny needle and ball.

At some time past midnight, she became aware of an added menace: from a broken weld in the manifold ring of the motor exhaust, flames were streaming. It was not immediately dangerous, but if the other sections became loosened by the engine's vibrations, the motor might explode because the fumes could not escape. Amelia faced the terror of death in a burning plane. She had passed the point of no return.

All her skill was needed to keep the plane on course. Icy wings alternated with dangerously low altitudes. The high rolling waves seemed almost to reach for her when she dived through the cold mists to free the wings of ice. As dawn came, the storm lessened in intensity, but Amelia knew she was using borrowed time with the flaming manifold. Ocean flying just before sunrise is often tantalizing and dangerous because of the occasional occurrence of mirages. As happened in the *Friendship* flight, Amelia "saw" land three times before her true landfall of the Irish coast. Peering over the side of the cockpit to try to gain an inkling of her location, she spotted some railroad tracks which she proceeded to follow until she was over a fair-sized city. Alas! There was no airport visible. She dared not risk more time in the air, so, banking sharply, she flew back a few miles to circle above a farm which she had noted had a smooth expanse of grazing land, not too thickly dotted by cows. Amelia set the weary Vega down in James Gallagher's pasture on the outskirts of Londonderry, Ireland, approximately fifteen hours after taking to the air at Harbor Grace.

Amelia's name was known to the Gallaghers, who made her heartily welcome. They summoned the constabulary to protect the plane until the manifold could be repaired and it could be flown to England, where it was placed on display in Selfridge's London store. Amelia used her twenty-dollar bill to cable GP. As soon as GP heard of Amelia's safe arrival he rushed from his New York office where he had spent the night, mentally flying with her. He reached the North River Pier just in time to get aboard the S. S. *Olympic* so he could keep his promised date with his wife in France.

From *Courage Is the Price*
by Muriel Earhart Morrissey

George Sand

George Sand (1804–1876), French novelist (born Amandine Aurore Lucie Dupin of an aristocratic father who died young and a mother who "came from the people"), spent her childhood and youth torn between two rival mothers, both strong yet selfish women who disliked each other and who brought out the worst in each: her mother and her paternal grandmother. More of her time was spent with her grandmother, yet she longed for her mother whom she described in her twenty-volume autobiography as "this ardent and unfortunate woman." Near the time of her grandmother's death, Sand wrote, "At last I could let my two rival mothers be intermingled in the same love. At that moment I felt I loved them equally, and hoped that I might prevail upon them to accept the idea." She couldn't. Of her mother, she was later to write, "And yet she loved me—or at least loved in me the memory of my father and my childhood; but also she hated in me the memory of my grandmother."

Although Sand grew up subject to family conflicts she did not emerge as scarred, but as a resilient and gifted woman well able to take care of herself. As a symbol of her rebellion from society's conventions, she wore men's clothing. She demanded for women the freedom of living that belonged to the men of her day.

After eight years of a marriage of convenience to Baron Dudevant she obtained a divorce. She lost her heart to several others, including Frederic Chopin. She spent the last years of her life back in the French countryside where because of her kindness she was known to the villagers as Notre Dame du Berry.

In her account of her school days one senses the strength and determination she possessed even as a child.

❋ MY grandmother had questioned a certain Mme. de Pontcarré about the English Convent, where she had been imprisoned briefly during the Revolution. One of Mme. de Pontcarré's nieces had been brought up in the convent and had just left it. My grandmama, who had certain not unpleasant memories of this monastery and of the nuns she had met there, was pleased to learn that the niece had been very well cared for and had received a refined education; it seemed that the girls were good scholars that the "masters of the polite arts" were renowned, and in sum, that the English Convent merited the vogue it then enjoyed in society, along with its rivals, Sacré-Coeur and the Abbaye-aux-Bois. Mme. de Pontcarré expected to place her own daughter there, which she did the next year. And so my grandmama decided that the English Convent was the very thing, and upon a winter day, I put on a uniform of purple serge, my school clothes were packed in a trunk, and we took a hackney to the Rue des Fossés-Saint-Victor. After we had waited some moments in the parlor, a communication door was opened, and then was closed behind us. I was encloistered. . . .

My first impression upon entering the lower form was distressing. About thirty of us were packed into a low, narrow room. A dreadful egg-yellow wallpaper, a dirty, decaying ceiling, filthy benches, desks and stools, a wretched, smoking stove, an odor of coal and poultry yard, an ugly plaster crucifix, a pitted floor—such was the place where we were to spend two-thirds of the day, three-fourths in winter. And just then it was winter.

Why our sisters, so beautiful, so kindhearted, and endowed with such noble and natural manners, had put at the head of the lower form a person of repellent bearing, countenance and dress, and of speech and character to match, I cannot fathom. Fat, dirty, stooped, bigoted, narrow, irascible, hard even to cruelty, suspicious, vindictive—she at once became the object of my moral and physical disgust, as she was already for all my companions.

There are natures to nobody's liking who keenly sense the aversion they excite, and who can never do good, even if they want to, because they lead others astray by their own sermonizing, and because they are reduced to "working out their own salvation" in isolation—the most sterile and irreligious thing in the world. Mlle. D. was such a nature. But it would be unfair of me not to tell her good points as well as her bad. She was genuinely pious and ruled herself with an iron hand; and she brought to her devotion a grim exaltation which made her intolerant and hateful, but which might have had a grandeur of sorts had she lived in the desert like the anchorites, whose faith she had. With us she became a dragon of rectitude; she derived joy from punishing, voluptuous pleasure from scolding, and in her mouth a rebuke was always an insult and an outrage. She was treacherous in her stern ways, and pretended to go out (which she should never have done during a lesson), just to overhear us speak ill of her and gleefully to catch us in the act of saying what we thought. Then she would punish us in the stupidest and most humiliating way. She forced us to cringe and fawn, and to kiss the ground for what she called our wicked words. This kissing of the ground was indeed a part of convent discipline, but the other nuns accepted a sham and pretended not to see when we kissed a hand as we bent toward the floor; whereas Mlle. D. pushed our heads into the dust, and would have broken them had we resisted.

It was easy to see what emotions lay behind her harshness, what rage she felt at being hated. In the class was a poor little English girl of five or six years, pale, delicate, sickly, a real *chacrot*, as we say in our Berrichon dialect to describe the frailest nestling in the brood. Her name was Mary Eyre, and Mlle. D. did her best to help her out and perhaps even to love her in a motherly way. But there was so little mother love in her mannish and brutish nature that she could not do it. Whenever D. scolded her she struck terror into her, or upset her to the point that she was soon forced, so as not to yield, to beat her or to lock her up. Sometimes she grew human enough to joke or try to play with her: but so might a bear have played with a sparrow. The little one would just keep on raging and screaming, out of sheer contrariness, or out of anger and despair. From dawn to dusk there was a nerve-racking contest, unbearable to watch, between the vicious fat woman and the sullen and unhappy little girl; but it did nothing to lessen the rigors and rages to which we were all in turn subjected.

I had wanted to enter the lower form out of a feeling of modesty not unusual in a child whose family is too vain; but I soon felt humiliated and offended by the rod of this old bogeyman in soiled petticoats. I had not been three days under her eye before I realized that I had to deal with a nature as violent as that of Rose, [a servant at home], but without Rose's frankness, affection and core of kindness. The first time her glance lit on me she said, "I should say you are a most dissipated young person," and from that moment on, I was ranked among her blackest sheep: for gaiety sickened her, children's laughter made her grind her teeth, and health, good humor—in a word, youth—all were crimes in her eyes.

The convent routine did not at all agree with me. We were decently fed—something I've never much cared about—but we suffered from the cruelest cold, and winter was very rigorous that year. The early bedtime hour was also as noxious to me as it was unpleasant. I've always liked to stay up late and not to rise early. At Nohant I'd had my way; I read and wrote in the evening in my room, and I wasn't forced to brave the morning chill. My circulation is slow—the word *sang-froid* perfectly describes both my moral and my physical constitution—but I was paralyzed by the cold, especially in the morning. The dormitory, situated in the attic under the roof, was so glacial that I could not fall asleep, and I would lie there sadly all night listening to the hourly bells. At six the servants Marie-Josèphe and Marie-Anne came pitilessly to wake us. To get up and dress by candle-light has always made me wretched. We had to break the ice in the ewers and the cold water did not clean us properly. We had chilblains, and our swollen feet bled in our tight shoes. We went to matins by candlelight and slept on our knees. At seven we breakfasted on a piece of bread and a cup of tea. Only when we finally entered the classroom did we see a faint light breaking in the sky and a little fire in the stove. I myself did not unfreeze till noon; I had frightful colds, and sharp pains in all my members; they plagued me for fifteen years thereafter.

Apathetic, mute, morose, I seemed in class to be the calmest and most submissive pupil. I had but one set-to with the ferocious D., which I shall describe anon. I never talked back, I never got angry, and I do not recall that I had the least crotchet during the three years that I spent at the convent. Thanks to this disposition, I made but one enemy, and that is the reason why I have kept a sort of grudge against D., who forced upon me the feeling most contrary to my nature. I was always liked, even in my most mischievous phase, and even by the sourest of my companions and severest of the mistresses and nuns. The mother superior told my mother that I was "standing water." Paris had chilled the feverish restlessness which had come over me at Nohant. But none of this stopped me from running on the roofs in December or from spending whole midwinter evenings bareheaded in the garden.

On the eve of my grandmother's departure from Paris, a storm brewed against me in the councils of the mother superior. I liked to write as much as I disliked to talk, and I amused myself by working the pupils' mischief and D.'s severities into a sort of satirical diary which I sent in installments to my grandmother, who was very amused by it; for she did not in the least commend fawning or docility, much less piety. Now, it was a convent rule that each evening we were to leave upon the cabinet in the mother superior's antechamber all the letters that we wished to have posted. Those not addressed to any relation were to be left open; those to our families were to be sealed, and their secrecy was supposed to be respected.

It would have been easy for me to convey my manuscripts to my grandmother using some more reliable go-between, since her servants often came to bring me things and to see how it was with me; but I had absolute faith in my superior's word. She had said to my grandmother in my presence that she never opened letters addressed to a pupil's family. I believed her, I trusted her, I never gave it a second thought. Yet the volume and frequency of my letters soon disquieted the "reverend mother." She unsealed them without ceremony, read my satires, and suppressed the letters. Three days running she did me this honor without saying a word, just to gain familiarity with my irreverent gazetteering and with D.'s manner of ruling over us. From these letters a woman of heart and intelligence would have learned a useful lesson—would have scolded me, perhaps, but would certainly have dismissed D. But then, a woman of heart would not have set a snare for a child's simple trust, nor invaded a privacy which she herself had authorized. The mother superior preferred to question Mlle. D., who of course failed to recognize herself in my accurate but unflattering portrait. And it was little wonder that her temper, already kindled by my calm air and manner, reached a speedy limit. She called me a "bald-faced liar," a "freethinker," and "informer," a "snake." The mother superior sent for me and caused a frightful row. I sat there like a stone. Then in her benevolence she promised me not to let my grandmother know of "calumnies" and to keep the secret of my abominable letters. But I saw the matter differently, and I sensed the duplicity of this promise. I replied that I had a draft of my letters, and that my grandmother would receive it; that I would uphold the truth of my assertions before my grandmother and before the "reverend mother" herself; and that since I could no longer put my faith in her word, I would ask to be placed in another convent.

The mother superior was not a wicked woman; but whatever one may think, I have never felt that she was a very good woman. She ordered me out, showering me with threats and insults. She was a person of standing in society, and she knew how to give herself royal airs when the need arose; but she sounded common indeed when she was angry. Perhaps she did not know how rank were the French expressions she was using (I did not yet know enough English for her to address me in her mother tongue). Mlle. D. only dropped her head and closed her eyes, and stood there in the ecstatic attitude of a saint listening to God's own voice, and when she looked at me she affected pitying airs and a compassionate silence. One hour later the mother superior entered the dining hall followed by a train of nuns; she reviewed each table as if making an inspection; then stopping before me and rolling her big black eyes, which were very fine, she said to me in a solemn voice:

"Practice the truth!"

The next moment I was deafened by questions from my fellow pupils.

"What this all means," I answered, "is that in three days I shall be gone."

I was indignant; but also very sad. I had no desire to change convents. I had formed bonds that I would suffer to see broken so soon. But at this point my grandmother arrived on the scene. The mother superior retired with her behind closed doors, and foreseeing that I would give everything away, thought best to pass my letters on to my grandmama and to present them as a tissue of lies. I suspect that she took quite a beating, and that my grandmother rebuked her sharply for the abuse of confidence she had been forced to divulge. Perhaps my grandmama even took my side and threatened to remove me straightaway. I don't know just what transpired between them, but when I was called into the mother superior's parlor, both were trying to look solemn, and both were very flushed. My grandmother kissed me as usual, and blamed me for nothing except for my laziness and for childishly rioting my time away. The mother superior announced that I was to leave the lower form and to enter at once the ranks

of the big girls. This good tiding, whereby so many threats co-
hered into a marked and irreversible improvement in my lot, was
nonetheless announced to me in a severe tone. It was to be hoped,
now that I was to have no more to do with Mlle. D., that I would
stop lampooning her, and that this separation would do us both
much good.

From *My Life* by George Sand

Florence Nightingale

The English mother of Florence Nightingale (1820–1910) thought her baby should bear the novel name of the city of her birth. Her personal fame was to become such that countless mothers would name their daughters after her. For a woman whose total aim in life was the care of the sick and of wounded soldiers, and who thus never shirked privation, she had a strange idea of modest living. Of the summer home of her childhood she said that it was only a small house. "Why," she declared, "it had only fifteen bedrooms."

That the nursing profession of her day could draw her is extraordinary. Its physically disgusting conditions were less an obstacle to her than the notorious immorality of hospital nurses. "It was preferred," she recognized, "that the nurses should be women who had lost their character. . . ." A physician of a large London hospital said in 1851 "the nurses are all drunkards." Their living conditions were hardly an inducement to sobriety. Ms. Nightingale described the sleeping conditions of a London hospital in 1854, "The nurses . . . slept in wooden cages on the landing places outside the doors of the wards, where it was impossible for the Night Nurse taking her rest in the day to sleep at all owing to the noise, where there was not light or air."

"The Lady with the Lamp," Florence Nightingale, turned all of this around. She made nursing a respectable, and even noble, profession. But not before, in spite of storms and lamentations on the part of her mother and sister, she went for a time to Kaiserwerth, Germany, to the Institute of Deaconesses where the religious atmosphere and ascetic discipline placed the nurses above suspicion; not before she and her unit of thirty-eight women gave legendary service to the wounded British soldiers in the Crimean

War; not before she established the Nightingale Training School for Nurses at Saint Thomas's Hospital in London.

❋

Kaiserwerth
(Letter to her mother)

ON Sunday I took the sick boys a long walk along the Rhine; two Sisters were with me to help me to keep order. They were all in ecstasies with the beauty of the scenery, and really I thought it very fine too in its way—the broad mass of waters flowing ever so slowly and calmly to their destination, and all that unvarying horizon—so like the slow, calm, earnest, meditative German character.

The world here fills my life with interest, and strengthens me in body and mind. I succeeded directly to an office, and am now in another, so that until yesterday I never had time even to send my things to the wash. We have ten minutes for each of our meals, of which we have four. We get up at 5; breakfast 1/4 before 6. The patients dine at 11; the Sisters at 12. We drink tea (*i.e.* a drink made of ground rye) between 2 and 3, and sup at 7. We have two ryes and two broths—ryes at 6 and 3, broths at 12 and 7; bread at the two former, vegetables at 12. Several evenings in the week we collect in the Great Hall for a Bible lesson. The Pastor sent for me once to give me some of his unexampled instructions; the man's wisdom and knowledge of human nature is wonderful; he has an instinctive acquaintance with every character in his place. Except that once I have only seen him in his rounds.

The operation to which Mrs. Bracebridge alludes was an amputation at which I was present, but which I did not mention to ———, knowing that she would see no more in my interest in it than the pleasure dirty boys have in playing in the puddles about a butcher's shop. I find the deepest interest in everything here, and am so well in body and mind. This is Life. Now I know what it is to live and to love life, and really I should be sorry now to leave life. I know you will be glad to hear this, dearest Mum. God has indeed made life rich in interests and blessings, and I wish for no other earth, no other world but this.

From *Letters to Mother,* edited by Charles Van Doren

Sarah Siddons

Discerning critics claim that Sarah Siddons (1755–1831) was the greatest English tragic actress of all times. Like Ellen Terry after her, she belonged to a family of strolling players, the famous Kemble family, and she began acting as a child. Her father, Roger, was an actor-manager, a courteous man, handsome and well-bred.

When almost seventeen, Sarah Kemble fell in love with William Siddons. Her parents were not pleased but by the time she was nineteen (and Siddons, twenty-nine) they permitted the wedding.

She was painted (or sketched) by Reynolds, Gainsborough, Romney, Gilbert Stuart, and Lawrence, among others. Thomas Lawrence, whose name was to be linked with her in calumnous attacks, remained her friend until his death. This friendship was the more remarkable when one realizes that seemingly he was in love with Sarah as well as with two of her daughters.

Hers was a complex character: "nervous, reserved, almost austere; restrained and cautious in real life, yet capable of the most violent and moving emotions on the stage." She spent herself exhaustively on the stage, and would sometimes return home from the theatre still weeping the real tears of her stage emotions.

In her final season, Sarah Siddons appeared in every part she had made famous by her interpretation, and on the last night of the season, June 22, 1812, it was as Lady Macbeth that she chose to retire from the London stage. When she walked off the stage after her last lines, the sleep-walking scene, the applause was so prolonged that the manager correctly concluded the audience wished the play stopped. When the curtain next rose, Mrs. Siddons was in her own clothes. She made her farewell speech and during its eight minutes there was profound silence.

At its finish there was again tumultous applause. She left the stage. Kemble came on stage to ask the audience if it wished the play to go on. They would not allow it to continue. Sarah Siddons had stopped the show.

In the years following her farewell Sarah Siddons did from time to time appear. An "appearance" which gave her great joy was the one she describes to a friend in this letter:

                    Westbourne, January 26, 1813

I HAVE been these three days meditating about writing you an account of my Windsor visit, which you have, no doubt, seen mentioned in the newspapers; but, whether occasioned by the fatigue of that visit, or from an habitual tendency, my head has been more heavy and painful since my return home than it has been for many months; but, though very far from well at present, I cannot resist the pleasure of telling you myself what I know you will be gratified to hear. Take it thus verbatim.

On the 18th (I think it was) I was in the middle of dressing to go and dine with Mrs. Damer, when an especial messenger arrived in the dusk, with a letter from my old friend the Dowager Lady Stewart, to tell me that the Queen had ordered her to write and say, "that her Majesty wished very much to hear me read, and desired to have an answer returned immediately to Carlton House, where the party from Windsor dined that day," which was Wednesday. I of course wrote that I should be happy to have the honour of obeying the Queen's commands, and therefore left my own house on Friday, according to appointment, and went to Frogmore, where I was informed that everything would be prepared for my arrival. I got there about three, and was conducted into a very elegant drawing-room, where I sat till it was time to go to the Castle, and consult with Lady Stewart respecting the reading. I spent about an hour very agreeably in her apartment with herself and Princess Elizabeth, who appears the best-natured person in the world. We concluded for some part of *Henry VIII.*, some part of the *Merchant of Venice,* and to finish with some scenes from *Hamlet*. After this I dined with Madame Bechendoft, her Majesty's confidential gentlewoman. When Lady Harcourt returned, after dining with the Queen, I again went to her apartment, where Princess Elizabeth renewed her visit, and stayed and chatted very charmingly, of course, because her conversation was chiefly about the pleasure they had all formerly received from my exertions, and the delight of hearing me again. We then parted for the night, the ladies to the Queen's card-party, and I to Frogmore, where the steward and housekeeper came to me, to say that her Majesty and the Princess had been there in the morning, and had left a message, to desire that I would consider myself as in my own house, with repeated injunctions to make my residence there as agreeable as possible. The next day the whole Royal party from Windsor, with Princess Charlotte and the Dukes of Cambridge and Clarence, dined at Frogmore. Many of the gentry and nobility were invited to the reading; and at about half-past eight I entered the room, where they were all assembled. The Queen, the Princesses, and the Duchess of York, all came to me, and conversed most graciously, till the Queen took her place. Then the company seated themselves, and I began. It all went well off to my heart's content, for the room was the finest place for the voice in the world. I retired, sometimes, at her Majesty's request, to rest; and, when it was over, I had the extreme satisfaction to find that they had been all extremely delighted. Lady Stewart wrote me yesterday, that I am still the inexhaustible fund of conversation and eulogium. When the Queen retired, after the reading, Lady Stewart brought to me a magnificent gold chain, with a cross of many-colored jewels, from her Majesty, and hung it about my neck before all the company. This was a great surprise, and you may imagine how so great an honour affected me. You may conceive, too, the pleasure it gave me, to be able to divert a few of those mournfully monotonous hours which these amiable sufferers, from the singularly afflicting nature of their misfortune, are doomed to undergo. I found that the Queen had been desirous that

I should not return the next day, but stay, and read again to her at the Castle next night, which I was too happy to do. This reading consisted of passages from *Paradise Lost,* Gray's *Elegy,* and *Marmion.* When I went into the room, I found her Majesty, with all the Princesses, and the Princess Charlotte, seated, and a table and chair prepared for me, which she (most graciously saying she was sure I must still feel fatigued from the last night's exertion) ordered me to seat myself in, when I thanked her for the magnificent favour I had received, and hoped the reading of the preceding night had not fatigued her Majesty, for she really had a terrible cough and cold. She hoped that the keepsake would remind me of Frogmore, and said "that it was impossible to be fatigued when she was so extremely delighted." I then took my leave, intending to return home the next day, which was Monday, but, having long meditated a short visit to Lord and Lady Harcourt, who live at St. Leonard's Hill, about four miles from Frogmore, I called there, and Lady Harcourt persuaded me to remain with her, and was so good as to make me send for Cecilia and Miss Wilkinson. While I was there I received another command from her Majesty; and the next Sunday evening I read *Othello* to the Royal party at the Castle: and here my story ends. I have much to say if I had eyes and head; my heart, however, is still strong, and I am, with undiminished affection.

Yours, S. S.

From *The Life of Mrs. Siddons* by Thomas Campbell

Anne Boleyn

Anne Boleyn (1507–1536) was the second queen consort of Henry VIII, for whom he divorced Queen Catherine of Aragon and by whom he hoped to have a male heir. Henry's love letters to her, which are now in the Vatican Library (of all places) reveal little beyond that she kept him waiting for a year. Openly infatuated with Anne, he saw in her a vivacious, witty woman of twenty-four, educated in France, with beautiful black eyes and thick black hair long enough to sit upon. The Venetian Ambassador saw something else. He wrote, "Mistress Anne is not the handsomest woman in the world. She is of middle height, dark-skinned, long neck, wide mouth, rather flat-chested."

Upon her failure to produce a male heir, Henry became disenchanted, which for him was tantamount to looking for a new enchantress. He found one in Jane Seymour. Anne was arrested and charged, among other offenses, with being unfaithful to the King. Although she denied each charge in detail she was declared guilty by a court presided over by her uncle, Thomas Howard, Duke of Norfolk, and was sentenced to death. She received her sentence with calm and courage.

In his History of the English-Speaking Peoples, *Winston Churchill tells of her last hours. She appeared for her execution in a robe of heavy, grey damask trimmed with fur and beneath which was a crimson kirtle. She had chosen this attire in order to leave her neck bare. Money had been given to her to distribute in alms among the crowd. "I am not here," she said, "to preach to you, but to die. Pray for the King for he is a good man and has treated me as well as could be."*

She removed her pearl-covered headdress revealing that her hair had been carefully bound up to avoid impeding the executioner (or perhaps she felt like Thomas More who arranged his beard to miss the executioner's blade, since it "had committed no treason."). "Pray for me," she asked and knelt down while one of the ladies-in-waiting bandaged her eyes. "God have mercy on my soul" were her last words, and the executioner with a single stroke performed his task.

Anne Boleyn produced no male heir but she was the mother of Elizabeth I, one of England's most able monarchs.

Here is one of her letters to Henry.

6 May, 1536

SIR, Your Grace's Displeasure, and my Imprisonment, are Things so strange unto me, as what to Write, or what to Excuse, I am altogether ignorant. Whereas you send unto me (willing me to confess a Truth, and to obtain your Favour) by such an one whom you know to be mine ancient professed Enemy; I no sooner received this message by him, than I rightly conceived your Meaning; and if, as you say, confessing a Truth indeed may procure my safety, I shall with all Willingness and Duty perform your Command.

But let not your Grace ever imagine that your poor Wife will ever be brought to acknowledge a Fault, where not so much as a Thought thereof proceeded. And to speak a truth, never Prince had Wife more Loyal in all Duty, and in all true Affection, than you have ever found in *Anne Boleyn,* with which Name and Place I could willingly have contented my self, if God, and your Grace's Pleasure had been so pleased. Neither did I at any time so far forget my self in my Exaltation, or received Queenship, but that I always looked for such an Alteration as now I find; for the ground of my Preferment being on no surer Foundation than your Grace's Fancy, the least Alteration, I knew, was fit and sufficient to draw that Fancy to some other Subject. You have chosen me, from a low Estate, to be your Queen and Companion, far beyond my Desert or Desire. If then you found me worthy of

248/ MOMENTS TO REMEMBER

such Honour, Good your Grace let not any light Fancy, or bad Counsel of mine enemies, withdraw Princely Favour from me; neither let that Stain, that unworthy Stain of a Disloyal Heart towards your good Grace, ever cast so foul a Blot on your most Dutiful Wife, and the Infant Princess your Daughter.

Try me good King, but let me have a Lawful Trial, and let not my sworn Enemies sit as my Accusers and Judges; yea, let me receive an open Trial, for my Truth shall fear no open shame; then shall you see, either mine Innocency cleared, your Suspicion and Conscience satisfied, the Ignominy and Slander of the World stopped, or my Guilt openly declared. So that whatsoever God or you may determine of me, your Grace may be freed from an open Censure; and mine Offence being so lawfully proved, your Grace is at liberty, both before God and man, not only to execute worthy Punishment on me as an unlawful Wife, but to follow your Affection already settled on that Party, for whose sake I am now as I am, whose Name I could some good while since have pointed unto: Your Grace being not ignorant of my Suspicion therein.

But if you have already determined of me, and that not only my Death, but an Infamous Slander must bring you the enjoying of your desired Happiness; then I desire of God, that he will pardon your great Sin therein, and likewise mine Enemies, the Instruments thereof; and that he will not call you to a strict Account for your unprincely and cruel usage of me, at his General Judgment-Seat, where both you and my self must shortly appear, and in whose Judgment, I doubt not, (whatsoever the World may think of me) mine Innocence shall be openly known, and sufficiently cleared.

My last and only Request shall be, That my self may only bear the Burthen of your Grace's Displeasure, and that it may not touch the Innocent Souls of those poor Gentlemen, who (as I understand) are likewise in strait Imprisonment for my sake. If ever I have found favour in your Sight; if ever the Name of *Anne*

Boleyn hath been pleasing in your Ears, then let me obtain this Request; and I will so leave to trouble your Grace any further, with mine earnest Prayers to the Trinity to have your Grace in his good keeping, and to direct you in all your Actions. From my doleful Prison in the *Tower,* this 6th of *May.*

Your most Loyal and ever Faithful Wife,
Anne Boleyn

From *Renaissance Letters: Revelations of a World Reborn,* edited by Robert J. Clements and Lorna Levant.

Cornelia Otis Skinner

Cornelia Otis Skinner (1901–1979) once said, "Inevitably some-one asks me what I do in my spare time. I can't answer that question because I never have any spare time." Educated at Bryn Mawr, the Sorbonne, and the Comédie Française, Ms. Skinner's life thereafter was divided between acting and writing. She won fame particularly for her one-woman shows and monologues. Several of her books became best-sellers. Her father, Otis Skinner, was a well-known actor; her mother stopped acting not long after Cornelia was born.

Before she was born (in Chicago) it was a foregone conclusion that she would be a girl and named Cornelia after her father's mother. Not long after Cornelia's birth her parents took her east in a market basket so that her Grandfather Skinner, a New England clergyman, would have the joy of baptizing her Cornelia after his wife. After the christening, however, he announced in ringing tones that there was no name he despised as much as that of Cornelia, and that although he had conferred it, with the Almighty as his witness, upon his granddaughter he would never call her by it. His loathing for the name went back to schooldays when as a small boy he had to share a desk with a girl named Cornelia who was disagreeable, a tattletale, and smelled. He never called his own wife anything but "Carrie."

To his granddaughter he gave the nickname "Bobs" because her head at that time seemed to him to bobble, and by that name she was known to family and some intimate friends. It was, however, as Cornelia Otis Skinner that she won audiences and readers with her charm, wit, and joy of living.

✳ IT was heartwarming to attend a recent sailing of that festive craft the *S.S. Vulcania,* bound from New York to Naples with a passenger complement that was nostalgically prewar in character. There were the same wanly exhausted Americans, the same Italians being exuberantly typical, the same wildly running children hurtling themselves into the same gentle-eyed stewards. The same pair of nuns stood apart discreetly whispering and the same energetic priests paced the decks with the same determined vigor. The familiar scene of amiable pandemonium quickened my sentimental pulse, and I found myself thinking back to breathless girlhood trips abroad, when Italy meant culture and fleas, *gelati* and *carabinieri* officers, tooled-leather picture frames and, if you had anything left on your letter of credit, a tea gown from Fortuny.

Perhaps it was the glimpse of the black-robed clergy, presumably on their way to receive the papal blessing, that put me especially in mind of Rome and of a pilgrimage made by my mother, my father, and myself to the Eternal City during the mid-nineteen-twenties. It was part of the parental scheme for my educational and spiritual improvement that, if possible, we should achieve the privilege of having an audience with the Pope. None of us knew exactly how to go about getting it, for we were not of the Faith. Indeed, it would have been difficult to define just what the family faith was. Mother, baptized a Catholic but for some reason not brought up as one, wavered between the Episcopal church, "because such nice people went there," and Ethical Culture, "because of that wonderful Dr. Adler"; Father, although he was the son of a Universalist preacher, adapted himself with an actor's sense of theatre to whatever church, temple, or even mosque in which he chanced to find himself, not that he very often did; while I, being at the time desperately in love with an actor, who was an ardent Christian Scientist, was immersed in Mary Baker Eddy. My father, through his friends in the Catholic Actors Guild, was able to pull a few ecclesiastical wires, and we ended up with an official letter introducing the Skinner family to the head of the American College in Rome. The fact that the letter was from Cardinal Hayes awed us all. Mother put it in our passport for safekeeping, which meant that it got lost quite often, because Mother was always finding new places where our passport could be successfully hidden from everybody, including herself. The morning we arrived in Rome, she fished it out of the bottom of my overnight case, in which, we discovered, a bottle of Chanel's Gardenia had come unstoppered. The letter reeked less of odor of sanctity than of the sort of sachet you send your cousin at Christmas. But since our stay in Rome was to be brief, Mother decided to present the letter that afternoon. We aired it out as best we could, and by the time the three of us turned up at the American College, Mother had optimistically concluded that whoever read it would think it smelled of incense. A handsome monsignor received us with cordial dignity, read the pungent communication without dilating a nostril, and told us he would be most happy to arrange for an audience; it might take a few days—he couldn't say how many—but in due course we would receive our formal invitation from the Vatican. Father thanked him. So did Mother, and then she said with a distressed flutter. "I think Your Reverence should know that we're not Catholics. But," she added brightly, "we'd all like to be!" The monsignor smiled warmly at Mother. However, he also closed the interview abruptly. Possibly he figured there would hardly be time for him to teach us our catechism prior to our audience. With a few kindly assurances to the effect that the papal benediction could extend even to such heretics as we, he politely saw us to the door. We clambered into a *carrozza* with the pious expressions of choirboys under the appraising eye of a deacon, and, sitting very upright, were driven back to our hotel, where, with the aid of a few Americanos sipped in the loggia to the strains of "Valencia," we relaxed into our habitual and more secular manner.

Some two hours later, as Mother and Father and I were assembled in the sitting room of our hotel suite just before dinner, there came an impressive knock on the door, which I opened to admit a gigantic and still more impressive individual, startlingly clad in the Michelangelo costume of the Papal Guard. At the sight of this magnificent blue, red, and yellow creature in striped doublet and hose, I gasped, Mother uttered a breathless "My!," and Father came out with a clarion "Good God!" The dazzling giant handed Father an envelope embossed with the Vatican seal, said something about the Pope, bowed and departed. Father opened the envelope, took out a heavy card exquisite with engraving and Spencerian penmanship, and, after studying it for some time, handed it to Mother with the excuse that he didn't have his glasses. Mother also studied it for quite a while, then looked up with the triumphant expression of someone who has just broken the enemy code and said, "Why, it's perfectly simple. It's in Latin." Father asked her what it said if it was so simple, to which Mother replied that she hadn't the slightest idea. "But," she said with maternal pride, "Cornelia's just had two years at Bryn Mawr," and passed the card on to me. My last practice in Latin had been the memorizing of an English trot of "The Aeneid," which hadn't exactly equipped me for such a social emergency as now confronted me. "This may take a little time," I said, and retired to the bedroom to do my homework. Be it to the glory of Bryn Mawr that it took only some fifteen concentrated minutes for my Latin to come back to me (there wasn't much to come), and I returned to my parents with the information that our audience was set for the following morning at eleven-thirty.

This didn't give us much time in which to make our preparations—not that we had the least idea what preparations to make. We were aware that there were strict regulations about clothes, but were quite vague as to what they were. Mother gave a little moan and said oh, dear, what a pity it was we weren't Catholics, an observation she was to repeat at periodic intervals during the ensuing eighteen hours. We consulted the hotel manager, to whom the dilemma of untutored American Protestants, it turned out, was an old and pretty uninteresting story. The Signor, he explained wearily, could wear a smoking (dinner jacket and black tie); the Signora must wear all black—high neck, long sleeves, head covering of a black veil; the Signorina likewise. Or the Signorina might, if she chose, go in all white, as she was still— and he coughed discreetly—a signorina. This observation I considered highly insulting. I was going through my F. Scott Fitzgerald period, and it infuriated me to be considered a virgin, especially when it was perfectly true.

After dinner, we started checking over our individual attire. Father's dinner clothes offered no problem, of course, and Mother claimed that my white tailored sports dress would do nicely, augmented with a lace mantilla I had acquired (after seeing Lila Lee wearing one in a movie). I was anything but enthusiastic about this spotless raiment and, when I eventually wore it, did so with an expression that I hoped implied there was more in it than met the eye. Outfitting Mother was more involved. The only black dress she had with her had a low-cut neck, elbow-length sleeve, and was trimmed with a bright beaded belt, which, in the grotesque fashion of the nineteen-twenties, struck her somewhere between the knees and the bottom of her round little rump. The hotel manager had informed us that there was a shop near St. Peter's where they rented out second-hand black raincoats to serve in an emergency, but when Father and I suggested the raincoat solution, she turned it down, saying she didn't think a raincoat would be reverent. No amount of pinning, it turned out would close up the space that disclosed a considerable expanse of her pretty neck. Father replied that he didn't know but that the regulations called for long sleeves, and he closed the argument with the actor's phrase of last resort: "You'll have to fake it." Mother asked what with, and, in a tone of finality, Father answered, "Stuff."

We had no vestige of "stuff" on hand, of course, so the only thing to do was to go out early next morning and buy some. Leaving Father behind with instructions to get into his dinner clothes, Mother and I set out in a taxi. After we had tried three department stores and found them all closed, our driver offered the explanation that this was Monday and that no shops opened before noon. He was quite indifferent to our distress until I explained that we were due for a papal *udienza* and that we could not possibly go unless we obtained some black material with which to fill my mother's neck. I think I said, in my halting Italian, "With which to stuff down my mother's throat," but he got the idea and was instantly all helpfulness. He had a friend in the Jewish quarter, he said, and the shops there were open, so he drove us to the establishment of an amiable little orthodox merchant who obligingly supplied us with two yards of nun's veiling. Halfway back to the hotel, Mother suddenly remembered her Catholic acquaintances, who were legion, and who, she said, would all be hurt if she didn't bring them rosaries blessed by the Pope. She had the taxi stop by a catchpenny pavement booth and, from a conglomeration of mosaic pins and alabaster reproductions of Cupid and Psyche, was able to extricate some two dozen rosaries. The vender, deaf to our protests that we were in a hurry and didn't want them wrapped, insisted upon doing up each one in a little twist of brownish tissue paper, like pieces of salt-water taffy. By the time we got back to our rooms, it was after ten-thirty. Father, still in drawers and undershirt, was postponing until the last possible moment the embarrassment of putting on a dinner jacket at such a peculiar hour. Mother panted at him for heaven's sake to hurry and get into his clothes, and at the same time hurried to get out of hers. With a scant half hour to go, the only possible thing to do was for Mother to put on her black dress and stand while I sewed in the necessary modesties. Dressmaking, unlike Latin, was not one of the equipments for life Bryn Mawr had given me. However, I went to work as best I could, seriously handicapped by Mother's inability to remain stationary. The chief cause of her fidgeting was Father, who was still wandering about in a state of unhappiness and seminudity. It seemed he could not locate his studs. Mother suggested a number of likely and unlikely places, but in the end he had to resort to a couple of brass clips pried from the manuscript of his next season's play. Mother thought this somewhat profane, but Father said not at all; it might prove very auspicious.

By dint of some rather cavalier basting and folding under of raw edges, I managed to change Mother's shameless neckline into a demure dickey. My reformation of the forearms was less chic. All I could do was to sew on some floating attachments that looked like dangling lining. However, we felt hopeful that she would pass the papal censor, except, perhaps, for the belt of colored beadwork. This was firmly attached to the dress. It seemed a pity to rip it off. On the other hand, it would be a greater pity if, because of such profane frippery, Mother should be barred from the audience. She decided to leave the belt as it was but also, "just in case," to take along some scissors. It was Father who did the carrying, the only available scissors being a pair too large for Mother's handbag. Father patiently tucked them in his dinner-jacket pocket.

Minutes were fleeting and I still had a few gaps to stitch up. Mother, for some time, had been urging Father to go down and engage a *carrozza*—a taxi, she felt, would not be sufficiently reverent—and Father kept finding excuses to putter around the room. Finally, mustering her utmost vehemence, she turned on him and wailed in a fluting tremolo, "Otis, why *don't* you go down and get us a *carrozza?*"

"If you must know, Maud," my father snapped, "I'm afraid someone'll mistake me for a waiter!," and he strode from the room.

I finished sewing Mother in, and we adjusted our respective veils and hastened down to a waiting open carriage, in which my father sat, looking uncomfortable and, to tell the simple truth, remarkably like a waiter. As mother and I settled ourselves beside him, we noticed he was wearing a pair of black cotton gloves. At sight of them, Mother giggled hysterically and asked what they were for and where he had ever got them. He replied that he had brought them along especially for this occasion and that he'd got them back in 1919, when he had served as a pallbearer in the funeral of a theatrical manager. Mother's mirth must have weakened his confidence in them, for he took them off, with injured dignity, and stuffed them in his pocket along with the scissors. We gave our imposing address to the driver, who, upon hearing it, paid tribute to the solemnity of the occasion by whipping up his horse and whisking us down the Corso and over the Tiber with the speed of a bat out of hell.

Clinging to the armrests of the careening vehicle, we came to a stop with a violent jerk before the Vatican doors. Two gorgeous guards admitted us and turned us over to a third, who led us through a labyrinth of marble corridors. Mother began making the little cooing noises she emitted whenever she felt that Father and I were about to do something that would shame us all, and repeated her comment about oh, dear, what a pity it was we weren't Catholics. Then she remembered her collection of rosaries and started taking them out of her bag. They were still done up in the salt-water-taffy twists. Feeling that this covering might insulate the beads against proper blessing, she carefully undid each one and hung it on her arm. Then, there being no wastebaskets around the Vatican, the question arose of how to dispose of the pieces of paper. Mother solved it by doing them up into two puffy wads and handing them to Father with a bland "Here, dear love." Father jammed them into his pockets along with the shears and the black cotton gloves. The pockets of his dinner jacket were beginning to take on the appearance of saddlebags.

Our letter from Cardinal Hayes had gained us the special distinction of a semi-private audience, apart from the larger devotional crowd. We were ushered into a small salon, the only other occupants of which were two very lovely-looking nuns, obviously persons of considerable ecclesiastical importance.

Mother whispered that they were mother superiors (I wondered how she knew) and that we must watch them closely and do whatever they did. It didn't seem too practical a suggestion, as at the moment both were engaged in intent perusals of their prayer books and we didn't even have a Baedeker between us. Mother compromised by folding her hands before her and staring at them with pious concentration. This embarrassed Father, who put on his reading glasses and walked about the room examining the pictures in a manner of self-conscious Protestant indifference that in turn embarrassed me. I stood apart, pretending I didn't know either of my parents very well. We had not long to wait before a uniformed official appeared bearing a sort of Malvolio staff, hastily herded the five of us into a row, and told us to get on our knees. Somehow, in the confusion, the Skinners got separated, so the final lineup, reading from right to left, turned out to be, first, Father, then a nun, then myself, then the other nun, and, finally, Mother, looking more nunlike than the authentic ones. The doors at the right opened, and the Pope, wonderfully magnificent in white, made a truly impressive entrance. He took us in with a brief glance, gave what I presume was a general blessing, then approached us individually, beginning with Father, who, I was shamed to note, received his benediction with head not bowed in piety but raised in an attitude of attention. I was further mortified to note that when His Holiness extended the great ring, my father, instead of kissing it, politely shook hands. The next blessing-recipient was one of the mother superiors, who, with beautiful grace, reached for the gloved fingertip, kissing the ring, crossed herself, and made appropriate response in devotional Latin. It then being my turn, I tried to do as she had done, but in my nervousness I must have clutched the papal hand too intensely, for just as I was about to kiss the ring, it was yanked away and the heavy jewel came in contact with an upper tooth, from which it excised a neat chip. Horrifying as this was, I did not feel that "I beg your pardon!" was the thing to say at the moment; nor did I think it would be seemly to try to salvage the piece of tooth from where it lay on the floor. I let it go as an act of penance. The Pontiff went on with some haste to the second mother superior, who reacted with the same exquisite dedication as her fellow-sister. He then paused before Mother. She kissed the ring most charmingly, crossed herself, and lifted her head in the manner of St. Cecilia having a vision. The Pope spoke his words of benediction and, to my amazement, I heard Mother responding with a stream of little unintelligible sounds—not words, exactly, just low, musical syllables. I thought perhaps the awesomeness of the ceremony had overworked her volatile emotions and that she had temporarily gone a bit daft. However, the Pope did not appear to think so. He paused, listened, smiled, and gave her an additional blessing before continuing on to other devotees, in the adjoining room.

As soon as we got outside, I asked Mother what on earth it was she had said in her response. "Nothing," she answered. "It was just because I was so ashamed of us all. There those two nuns were, looking so lovely and saying such beautiful things in Latin and we Skinners looking so hick and saying nothing, so I decided to make noises that sounded like Latin, and if the Pope didn't understand, he'd put it down to an American accent. But I think he understood." And the curious thing is I believe he did.

From *A Family Blessing*
by Cornelia Otis Skinner